Twayne's United States Authors Series

EDITOR OF THIS VOLUME

Warren French

Indiana University

Paul Goodman

TUSAS 358

PAUL GOODMAN

By Kingsley Widmer

TWAYNE PUBLISHERS
A DIVISION OF G. K. HALL & CO., BOSTON

Copyright © 1980 by G. K. Hall & Co.

Published in 1980 by Twayne Publishers,
A Division of G. K. Hall & Co.
All Rights Reserved

Printed on permanent/durable acid-free paper and bound
in the United States of America

First Printing

Library of Congress Cataloging in Publication Data

Widmer, Kingsley, 1925–
Paul Goodman.

(Twayne's United States authors series; TUSAS 358)
Bibliography: p. 176–79
Includes index.
1.   Goodman, Paul, 1911–1972
—Criticism and interpretation.
PS3513.0527Z95   818'.5'209   79–24479
ISBN 0-8057-7292-8

S
35/3
J527
29

Contents

About the Author

Preface

Chronology

1. The Man of Letters   17

2. The Conservative Anarchist   37

3. The Therapeutic Gadfly   65

4. The Literary Hobbyist   106

5. Conclusion: The Libertarian Legacy   144

Notes and References   151

Selected Bibliography   176

Index   180

About the Author

Kingsley Widmer was raised in midwestern small towns and schooled at the Universities of Wisconsin, Minnesota, and Washington (Ph.D.). He considers as an essential part of his education a variety of jobs—field hand, merchant seaman, construction worker, infantry soldier, template maker, convict, and so on—and his intermittent libertarian activities. Professor Widmer has taught at Reed College and the Universities of Minnesota, Washington, California (Berkeley), Tel Aviv (Israel), Simon Fraser (Canada), Nice (France), New York (Buffalo), Tulsa, and, for many years, San Diego State. He has published radical social critiques and poetry as well as half a dozen volumes of literary-cultural criticism, including *The Art of Perversity: D. H. Lawrence's Shorter Fictions, Henry Miller, The Literary Rebel, The Ways of Nihilism: Melville's Short Novels, The End of Culture: Essays on Sensibility in Contemporary Society,* and many uncollected essays in periodicals. Currently he lives at the beach in southern California and is working on several books—on literary modernism, of poetry, and on libertarian thought.

Preface

By chance, I first read an essay by Paul Goodman in Dwight MacDonald's left-libertarian *Politics* toward the end of World War II. I recall being both stimulated and irritated by the piece, and that response to Goodman's writings has not essentially changed in thirty-odd years, though I hope my ability to explain it has improved a bit. When I first read Goodman I was a nineteen-year-old disgruntled infantry private, anomalously assigned, before going into line-combat in Europe, to prepare lectures and displays for infantry companies on "Why We Fight." The job helped educate me, in disillusioning experiences as well as in access to a curious range of reading materials, as to which wars I would, and wouldn't, fight. After the army, and engaged in fighting other stupid institutions, I read more of Goodman—polemics, *Art and Social Nature*, sketches, a novel. I must suppose he was one of the intellectual influences which led to my symbolic defiance of U. S. militarism and to prison service as a felon in 1948–1949. Goodman appears to have had some parallel influence on others, especially some years later.

I spent an evening with Paul Goodman in 1950 and found his literary views arrogantly arbitrary, and his humorless egotism and compulsive sexuality unpleasant. Still, as an energetic graduate student in literary New Criticism, I was prepared to separate the personality and the writings, or at least to balance out the character disorders and the intellectual stimulation. It was not, and is not, necessary to like the man personally to find some of his writings provocative and significant.

Continuing to read Goodman, in the early 1960s I wrote a critical essay on him as a failed literary rebel, eventually published in my *The Literary Rebel* (1965). In the middle 1960s I helped arrange for Goodman to give some lectures at San Diego State College, though I avoided meeting him again. In later years, I taught some of Goodman at a college and at a "Free

University," wrote argumentative pieces about his current writings for the New York *Village Voice* and the London monthly *Anarchy*, and, with Eleanor Rackow, revised one of his essays (with the author's permission) for inclusion in an anthology, *Freedom and Culture* (1970). After Goodman's death in 1972, I wrote a review-essay around his last book for the *Nation*. The then literary editor didn't like my views or manners, "misplaced" my detailed justifications which he had asked for, and finally published a reduced version of my piece (reprinted with other material in my *The End of Culture*, 1975), soon followed by a more purely laudatory piece by a Goodman protégé. That ended my several-year role as a contributor to that periodical but not my interest in the subject, whom I continued to find useful to draw upon in various lectures and writings on anarchism. Though always aware that Goodman was a muddy writer, an often muddled thinker, and probably not historically a major figure, I felt that parts of his writings, amidst a great quantity of failed and bad work, had some continuing pertinence as an expression of certain libertarian attitudes and of some dissenting, and perplexing, roles of the American literary intellectual.

This information should suggest to the reader some of my biases toward the subject. However, it is not just my earlier responses to Goodman but a general critical insistence which continues to apply here. Half a dozen books ago I quoted D. H. Lawrence, when reviewing a scholarly work, back at him: "The author refused to take an attitude, except that of impartiality, which is the worst of all attitudes." I don't make that mistake, at least, and try to practice criticism as criticism—the attempts at discriminations, arguments with the subject matter and the world, and human judgments. Not to do so is pernicious intellectual time-serving.

In an earlier book for this series, *Henry Miller*, I practiced some hard-nosed criticism, which seemed irrelevant to those who disdained the subject and offensive to those who worshiped him (including Henry Miller). While I won't repeat my answers to the hate-letters, two learned objectors might be quoted: "Why write a book about someone you don't altogether admire?" Because intellectual engagement must be something other than hagiography. Otherwise it is not properly human. "Does the world need another negative portrait of the artist?" Certainly, if art is of any real concern, for we should respond to what is rather than give in to mere piety and positiveness. Though Goodman did not clearly recognize it, his talents and his utilities were mostly those of the iconoclast. He deserves appropriate response.

Still, I have often turned a bit to quote Goodman at his best rather than his frequent worst—not to be tiresome—and to ignore some contradictions, muddles and ugliness, and to suggest a coherence which is sometimes not altogether present. Some of that, of course, is inevitable to critical selectivity, which is necessarily drastic with Goodman's forty or so volumes of stories, poems, novels, plays, autobiography, letters, political arguments, movie and TV criticism, psychological theorizing, speculations on urban planning, educational polemics, aesthetics, prayers, linguistics, literary criticism, historical projections, moral philosophy, and yet other matters which came to his intense and earnest attention as a teacher, therapist, dissenter, bohemian, bisexual apologist, and broad Man of Letters with many publishing possibilities. While Goodman made much of his literary roles as poet, novelist, dramatist, and critic, which he apparently felt sanctioned his dissident roles and living, justice requires emphasis upon him as a failed litterateur who was a suggestive conservative anarchist and an important libertarian social iconoclast. Thus, after the first chapter's introduction to the figure and some of his roles as a Man of Letters, I examine his libertarian views in two long chapters—especially focusing on his important ideologies of education and decentralizing—before turning to his various literary efforts. The biography is only brought in (especially in the first and fourth chapters) as part-explanation of his peculiarity.

I hope my discussion of Goodman's writings and attitudes equally displeases the devoted and the dismissive. I am indebted to some of both. Taylor Stoehr, though aware of my critical views, generously took time from his biography of Goodman to answer biblio-biographical questions. Some things I pleasantly learned in conversations over the years with some-time friends of Goodman's, especially Eleanor Rackow Widmer, the late Benjamin Nelson, and Sam Hardin. Other observers of Goodman provided curious anecdotes and suggestions but might prefer to remain anonymous. Warren French suggested this study and was, as he has been over the years, exceptionally helpful and tolerant. I owe much to Penny Williams for her encouragement and responsiveness. Except for the use of several university libraries, I was, as usual, in no way aided or abetted by any institution, its officials, monies, or ambience.

Paul Goodman's "Schultz, the neighbor's big black dog," is reprinted from *Collected Poems* (© 1973 by the Estate of Paul Goodman), with the kind permission of the publisher, Random House, Inc.

KINGSLEY WIDMER

Pacific Beach, California
1978

Editor's note: It should be acknowledged that this first comprehensive study of the literary career of the late Paul Goodman marks a departure from the customary tone of this series. This is a controversial account of Goodman's art and thought. Throughout his life Paul Goodman thrived on controversy. An inveterate protester, he also protested protest if others began too much to agree with him. To present an uncritical appreciation of his productions would be a disservice to his life-style.

Despite the volume of his publications, Goodman was also, for many people, a one book man. Like many others, I discovered him with *Growing Up Absurd*, which seemed to me as a college teacher in the 1950s to capture as exactly the desperate mood of my sensitive students as J. D. Salinger's novel *The Catcher in the Rye* had at the beginning of the decade. How much did Goodman influence the almost immediate turn of youth toward activism? Perhaps not at all. Perhaps his book was simply superbly timed. Like others, I turned to his further works with disappointment—he never again so exactly matched the temper of the moment.

Kingsley Widmer places Goodman's most popular work into a context of his many other polemics. Intrigued by the same kind of libertarian thinking that attracted Goodman, Widmer

Preface

is able to set up what amounts to a dialogue with a disembodied voice, documenting his analysis with detailed references to his subject's scattered pronouncements. Those who welcome bland syntheses may be distressed that this book bristles with notes; but the documentation here is no arid display of pedantry. It is rather a guide through the bewildering variety of Goodman's performances from the kind of sympathetic yet rigorously critical point of view that needs to be imposed upon the enthusiastic schemes and proclamations of anyone who sets out to save the world.

I have worked for more than a decade now with Kingsley Widmer, and I continue to marvel at the way he can marshal a case to lay before the jury of readers who must eventually arrive at their own verdicts.

To simplify somewhat, however, the tangled trail through Goodman's works, the following abbreviations are used in the text and notes to identify references to some of his most frequently cited books:

Absurd	— *Growing Up Absurd* (1960)
CP	— *Collected Poems* (1973)
Compulsory	— *Compulsory Mis-education* (1964)
Creator	— *Creator Spirit Come! The Literary Essays of Paul Goodman*, ed. Taylor Stoehr (1977)
Line	— *Drawing the Line: The Political Essays of Paul Goodman*, ed. Taylor Stoehr (1977, not the same as *Drawing the Line*, 1962)
Nature	— *Nature Heals: The Psychological Essays of Paul Goodman*, ed. Taylor Stoehr (1977)
People	— *People or Personnel* (1965)
Province	— *Like a Conquered Province* (1967)
Scholars	— *The Community of Scholars* (1962)
Society	— *The Society I Live In Is Mine* (1963)
Speaking	— *Speaking and Language* (1971)
Utopian	— *Utopian Essays and Practical Proposals* (1962)

W. F.

Chronology

1911 Paul Goodman born in New York City, 9 September, fourth child of Augusta and Barnett Goodman, American born of German-Jewish and middle-class origins. Failing in business, father abandoned family prior to birth. Sister Alice (1902–1969) partly raised, and later supported, her brother. Brother Percival (b. 1904), later architect and academic, collaborated on city writings. Mother, traveling saleswoman in ladies' wear, mostly left her son to be raised by her sisters and daughter, without father figure, in modest circumstances in New York City.

1916– Good student in public schools, excelled in literature and
1927 languages at Townsend Harris Hall High School (graduated 1927). Attended Hebrew school; identified with Manhattan.

1927– Good student at City College of New York; philosophy
1931 major (A.B., 1931); strongly influenced by philosopher Morris R. Cohen; lifelong friendships with fellow students who became academicians and writers, some part of his intellectual coterie.

1931– Determined only to be a writer, worked on stories and
1936 poems and plays; lived with sister; no regular employment. Audited graduate philosophy courses at Columbia. Summer job (1934–1936) as drama counselor at Zionist youth camp.

1936– Graduate student in literature and philosophy, University
1940 of Chicago; research assistant (1936–1937); part-time instructor in "Ideas and Methods" (1937–1939); passed qualifying exams in literature (1940). Active bisexual.

1940– Writing in New York; published by *Partisan Review* and
1943 New Directions. Common-law marriage to Virginia Miller (1938–1943); daughter Susan (b. 1939). First novel, *The Grand Piano* (1942).

1943– Taught at a progressive boarding school, Manumit; dis-
1944   missed for homosexual behavior. Deferred, then rejected, in World War II draft.

1945   Published collection of stories, *The Facts of Life*. Began writing for libertarian periodicals (*Politics*, *Why?*, *Retort*) and developing anarchist views. Began twenty-seven-year common-law marriage with Sally Duchsten (intermittent secretary).

1946   Birth of son, Mathew Ready. Published small book of anarchist and aesthetic essays, *Art and Social Nature*, and novel *State of Nature*. In psychoanalytic therapy. Well known in New York bohemian circles, living (as for next dozen years) in "marginal" style.

1947   Published critical study, *Kafka's Prayer*, and, with Percival, *Communitas*, on city planning.

1948– Writing in New York, published sketches based on earlier
1949   summer job, *The Break-Up of Our Camp* (1949).

1950– Additional psychoanalytic therapy, and intermittent prac-
1951   tice (until 1960) as paid therapist. Published *Gestalt Therapy*, with F. S. Perls and R. Hefferline (1951). Published, by subscription of friends, novel *The Dead of Spring* (1950), and novelized account of progressive school teaching, *Parents' Day* (1951). Taught at Black Mountain College; dropped for bisexual behavior.

1951– Writing, and practicing therapy, in New York City. Com-
1954   pleted doctoral dissertation in literature, University of Chicago, published as *The Structure of Literature* (1954).

1955– Writing and therapy in New York. Summer tour of western
1959   Europe (1957), spring tour of Ireland (1958). Published in varied journals (*Kenyon Review*, *Commentary*, *Dissent*, *Liberation*, of which he was an editor for some years). Published multiple novel, *The Empire City* (1959). Associated with Living Theatre (Beck-Malina), which produced some of his plays.

1960– Published *Growing Up Absurd*, topical social criticism,
1961   which made him famous and led to many lecturing and publishing opportunities and substantial income. Bought farm near North Stratford, New Hampshire, intermittent home for next dozen years. Published sketches, *Our Visit to Niagara*. Taught term at Sarah Lawrence.

Chronology

1962 Published criticism of academia, *The Community of Scholars*; first collected poems, *The Lordly Hudson*; and revised articles, *Utopian Essays and Practical Proposals*.

1963 Published memoir-novel, *Making Do*. Fellow of Institute for Policy Studies, Washington (1963–1965). Birth of daughter Daisy.

1964 Visiting Professor of Urban Affairs, University of Wisconsin, Milwaukee. Published *Compulsory Mis-education*. Active in protest movement.

1965 Published his major statement on decentralizing. *People or Personnel*; much journalism and lecturing.

1966 Student-appointed professor at San Francisco State (spring).

1967 Published polemical Canadian broadcasts of previous year, *Like a Conquered Province*; *Hawkweed* (verses). Lectured in London. Active in war protests and draft resistance. Only son, Mathew, killed in mountaineering accident, which led to years of depression. Published in many periodicals, including *N.Y. Review of Books* and *N. Y. Times*.

1968– *Adam and His Works*, stories (1968). Irregular aca-
1969 demic appointment at University of Hawaii.

1970 Published last book of social criticism, *New Reformation*.

1971– In poor health—cardiac condition. Another appointment at
1972 Hawaii. Published *Speaking and Language* (1971). Last jottings on religion and other matters, *Little Prayers & Finite Experience* (published posthumously, 1972). Worked on *Collected Poems* (published posthumously, 1973). Gave a few public lectures. Died of a heart attack August 2, 1972, in New Hampshire.

FOR MY FELLOW ANARCHISTS,
PAST AND PRESENT

CHAPTER 1

The Man of Letters

I   The Literary Life

PAUL Goodman devoted much of his life to literary work and
published much. However, the only sensible critical response
to most of it must conclude that he badly failed as a literary
artist. Of far more value were some of Goodman's roles as a
provocative critic of mid-twentieth-century American society.
Because of his social criticism he became, in middle age, a dissident figure of note in the 1960s as part of the protest movement—
spokesman for war resistance and student rebellion, an iconoclastic reformer and broad-ranging social gadfly. Some of his
social criticism, I believe, retains considerable intellectual value
as well as historical significance, especially some of his applied
libertarianism on education, roles of youth, community aesthetics,
anarchist resistance, and the radical functions of the Man of
Letters.

Goodman's was a rather "peculiar" character, by which I mean
something between "eccentric"—accurate but too mild—and "psychopath" (his label)[1]—also accurate but too clinical. His intensely
earnest contentiousness, his gross conceit, his flaunted bisexuality,[2] his offensive style (in his writings as well as in person),
were so blatant as to have some provocative charm. His conven-
tion-shocking avowals—given his times and audiences—included
anarchism, draft-dodging, early sex, banning the automobile,
abolishing much of schooling, and a number of sweeping schemes
for reordering American institutions. They seemed so extreme
to many as to be piquant, though they were often commonsensically qualified and importantly suggestive.

As a person, Paul Goodman was often highly charged intellectually yet ill-focused, partly because of a fracturing of
ideology by an earnestness which outran his seriousness, and by

personal obsessions.[3] He could be engaged in an emphatic philosophical argument yet simultaneously distracted to homosexual advances. His intellectualism usually seemed erotically compensatory. When young, he thought of his awkwardly nondescript "Jewish" appearance as homely; by his forties, he thought of himself as "terribly ugly."[4] He heightened it by tasteless sloppy dress, missing teeth (for many years), ill-fitting glasses (he was quite nearsighted), offensive mannerisms (drooling down a pipe-stem, scratching his backside, sexual leering and groping), and by unfastidious personal habits. "I like dirt,"[5] he rationalized, and with similar defensiveness he liked the sloppiness of his thinking and writing. He could be enthusiastically or tearfully responsive, yet quick with a contemptuous show of learning—a magisterial quotation from Kant or Buber, a smugly esoteric comparison, a dogmatically flung odd statistic—and the spiteful put-down. He seemed intellectually eager, personally concerned, emotionally unbuttoned, tremblingly physical, yet would quickly become obsessive, domineering, or sulky. In social scene or public performance, he often courted affection, flattery, sycophancy, yet insisted on interrupting, insulting, embarrassing, in quick switches from the winsome to the patronizing. He never grew out of the role of *enfant terrible* with a defensive adolescent conceit as a "genius" who was the "best" in all intellectual matters and the hostile domineering in which people had to be his followers.[6] In resentful reaction to a world which rejected him— and he took lack of lavish praise as rejection—his usual response, he said, was "to kick at it, to be spitefully utopian, to bawl."[7] Much of his thinking and writing were of a piece with this messy and awkward personality.

Certain early peculiarities contributed to the erratic character. Perhaps the crucial condition around Goodman's birth in 1911 was fatherlessness—his failing-businessman parent had abandoned his pregnant wife and three children. There appears not to have been a surrogate father (until his partial indentification later with some teachers) and the boy was raised with the help of maternal aunts and, later, a nine-year-older sister, since the mother was much away as a traveling saleswoman in ladies' wear. Apparently the youngest son was often alone as a child, which probably had something to do with his bookishness and strong performance in the public schools of Manhattan, as the erratically woman-dominated early environment had something to do with his homosexuality and contempt for females.

As fatherless Jean-Paul Sartre pointed out about himself, since he had no father he lacked the usual "super-ego" inhibitions.[8] Both Sartre and Goodman made up for it with a grandiose sense of literary role and a defiant sense of public political role. While Goodman was anxiously fatherless (no one, he complained, "to rebel against," and, "I had no guidance," *CP*, pp. 103, 409), and always thought of himself as homely, like Sartre, and similarly reacted with an obsessive verbalism, they were antithetical in the relations to the mother. If the account in the novel-memoir *Parents' Day* is accurate, Goodman and his mother were mostly antagonistic: "We could not stay in the same house, even in the same city, we riled each other so" (p. 140). This may have been the little boy's explanation of why she would repeatedly leave, and may have become self-fulfilling: "When I was a child, my mother threatened to abandon me, or did" ambivalently noted the later versifier (*CP*, p. 122). The sense of missing father and wandering mother may have encouraged the extreme and permanent anxiety in which "I could not endure a breath of rejection."[9] This led to the outrageous behavior which brought forth the rejection he was constantly expecting. Some such pattern must have been part of Goodman's markedly offensive adult style, including the fusion of the earnest and insulting in his writing. And it would have to be part of the repeated lament of being "in exile," otherwise inappropriate for a parochialist of a self-centered familial and coterie life (*CP*, p. 338, and elsewhere). Perhaps, too, this pervasive familial anxiety is part of his obsessive concern with familylike "community" in his social thought. This is less my genetic psychologizing than Goodman's own, since he pointed out that his social concerns were those of one "who has been maimed in his own upbringing, as I have" and who feels alienated "from group belonging"—unreasonably so.[10]

Feeling marginal in familial and social (declassed) roles, Goodman did competitively well in the public schools, especially in literature and languages at Townsend Harris Hall High School (graduated 1927), which served as something of a "prep" school for New York City College, viewed by some then as the New York Jewish "proletarian Harvard." Goodman majored in philosophy and minored in literature, performed well, made some of the lifelong friends who later aided him in his intellectual ambitions and financial needs, and graduated in 1931. Then for some years he made little effort at any career or securing regular employment, except for amateurish writing. Largely supported by his employed older sister, and psychologically by a coterie, he took up the literary life.

While the conditions of the Great Depression may have encouraged, in part, this role, it had other sources. Flattered by high-school English teachers and by college literary publication, Goodman saw writing as an exempting activity. The "creative" served for somewhat educated Americans for several generations— as it still does for some—as an escape from a tediously restrictive life and mean origins, an "out" for those who thought of themselves as physically and socially and economically "inept" (as Goodman did). He later wrote that he became a writer so as *not* to "choose a career." It was also insulation from a feared hostile world, a self-confirmation not open to criticism or rejection since he was convinced that at fifteen he wrote "just fine" and had "the total art," so he could simply dismiss, as he ever after did, most criticism and adverse response.[11] To be a "writer" was not only an exempting and honorific role; it could provide self-transcendence of self-hatred for the ugly and rejected emotional exile.

Goodman was aware of terrible inconsistencies in his behavior which he could override by playing the artist: "It was the picture of a creative artist that I was consistent with; and such a picture has more of the self in it than there exists in the self; it is what the self will make of the self."[12] Even toward the end of his life, he felt that the self-bootstrapping trick of playing the writer had worked: "What could have been a fragmented existence has become a regular and respected career."[13] The "abandoned one," the "lumpen bourgeois," the poor and inept Jewish boy, had made it into the magical world of the "professions" by claiming to be the Artist. With such psychological and social needs of recreating the self as Creative Writer, no mere questions of competence or response—or their lack—could be allowed to intrude upon the role, part of the "psychopathic adjustment" that Goodman claimed characterized artists (*CP*, pp. 104, 330). With this insular self-image, we can understand Goodman's imperceptivity about his own writings and perhaps much of his resentment toward most of his contemporary writers. Feeling outcast, and with this exacerbated by homosexuality and other peculiarities from the lack of super-ego inhibitions, an obsessive Jewish intellectual from his education and milieu, the bohemian writer-artist provided more than an occupation—a role, a literary community, a better self. We may take, with some psychological literalness, I think, the late verses on pressured role-playing: "Long I labored to make me Goodman," and, "to my surprise the face fits me . . ." (*CP*, p. 398). Whether it did or not, he was to stick to it with remarkable persistence, and not a little obtuseness, for four decades.

Paul Goodman also played some related roles: perennial student from the 1930s on (he finally completed a University of Chicago Ph.D. in literature in 1954); writer about and practitioner of a form of "gestalt" psychotherapy (through the 1950s); an intermittent teacher of several subjects—writing, literature, sociology (for perhaps a total of seven or eight years); and (from 1960 to his death in 1972) a much published social critic, traveling lecturer, public scold, and symbolic dissident. But some version or other of the literary life remained a constant self-definition—repeatedly referred to in lectures, smugly insisted on in his social criticism, and returned to as his primary concern in his last years as his gadfly role faltered.

Though Goodman probably did as much, and certainly better, social criticism as imaginative literature, there is some of the same obstinate perversity in all his intellectual roles. He defiantly preached an anarchism which often added up to liberal-reformism, or even an odd conservatism. His self-admitted—and then some!—"humiliating" compulsive homosexuality was part and even a technique, in his mind, of the exalted roles of teacher, therapist, and libertarian. His crude candor may have contributed to the Gay Liberation movement which arose in his last years.[14] Though self-consciously playing the bohemian apologist—that is the main concern of his half dozen novels—he was also, in his literary criticism and other arguments, em-

phatically a pedant *manqué*. While claiming the social place
of the intellectual arch-dissident and vanguardist, he was often
a gross neoclassicist and quaintly antique moralist. Part of his
stimulation and irritation may be due to the breakdown of usual
categories in responding to such curious mixtures of the conservative and the radical, the traditional and the outrageous, the
weirdly peculiar and the commonsensically suggestive.

Goodman became a fairly prolific writer, averaging in his later
life more than a book, of some sort, a year, in addition to much
periodical publication. Yet he usually wrote badly and did not
improve over the years. He tried quite a variety of forms—
tragedy and farce, learned essay and casual polemic, fable and
reportage, novel and anthology of lyric modes, sociology and
prayer, even musical composition and psychiatric manual, as
well as TV column and political manifesto.[15] Not only did he
not master the forms, but most of them—story, essay, lyric, play,
and so on—are marked by gross violations of point of view, pattern, tone, style. Yet, although almost always awkward and
disorganized, the writing often reaches the odd insight or scored
point. The reader is frequently left uncertain whether the bad
writing and thinking are the result of ignorance or defiance or
carelessness. Admitting that he was not an "expert" on many of
the subjects that he wrote about, he even insisted on his "ignorance" as well as naiveté and carelessness as if they were
special qualifying virtues. Yet, *lumpen* character that he was,
he also smugly relished knowing the experts and playing the
learned "professional" among other professionals.[16] However,
he wasn't truly knowledgeable, much less a master, on *any*
subject—on any literature or author, on Freudian theory, on
juvenile delinquency, on American universities, on anarchism,
or on other matters he turned to again and again. He did have
a good memory and a ruminative mind and an intellectual insistence, even on science, opera, medieval history, colonial
politics, picture framing, as well as on his more usual social and
literary concerns. He had little inhibition—that missing super-ego,
again?—in writing, as in speech, when it came to slapping together scattered bits of erudition for an aggressive argument
on Calvinistic theology, modern technological training, Populist
American history, contemporary painting, Chinese religion,

French verse forms, psychological experimentation, or whatever else he could paste together with a quotation from Aristotle, an example from Genet, a report from the Bureau of Labor Statistics, an aphorism from Kafka, an anecdote from a hustler or an historian, a sentence from Kropotkin or Jefferson. Little of this obsessional speaking-writing, which in spite of all the training and degrees has the tonalities of the autodidact, is quite truly learned, subtle, or original, yet repeatedly it turns a curious or intriguing point.

Goodman wrote poems for nearly half a century, and usually claimed "Poet" (or Artist) as his identity, yet had little sense of poetry and an absurdly wooden sense of language. He was professionally trained in philosophy by some rather rigorous teachers, yet he could rarely analyze a proposition or follow a line of argument very steadily. An avowed Enlightenment universalist, he was also a maudlin American patriot and a parochial localist, especially in the New Yorker sense, with its anxious alienation and ignorant provincialism. An extreme and harshly perceptive nay-sayer, he thought of himself as above all positive—he loved to sententiously repeat, "Nothing comes from nothing"[17]—and in his most sweeping denunciations he took himself to be a commonsensical yea-sayer making "practical proposals." As a helpful reformer, he often turned out to be an obstreperous social revolutionary; as a left-revolutionary activist, he lectured campus rebels on the medieval university, or insisted in protest politics on something "knightly" or "noble" or "citizenly." This was the stuff of comedy, but he had little humor and less wit. The very mélange, he seemed to think, made him a redemptively independent "humanist," a "Renaissance free-lance" Man of Letters, a latter-day Milton, a counselor to the miserable and the mighty, and a philosopher of the good life.[18] Perhaps it sometimes did.

Though certainly peculiar, Goodman clearly belongs to a time and place; he is hardly conceivable without the midcentury New York ambience. Though he lived a considerable part of his later years in New Hampshire, made four trips to Europe, taught in varied academic institutions (Chicago, Black Mountain, Wisconsin, San Francisco State, Hawaii), put in time in Washington, and lectured at hundreds of campuses and conferences, in intel-

lectual sensibility he never left Manhattan. In part he could
naively throw around his radical social proposals because he
could never believe in, much less understand, most of ordinary
America and its alienated and restrictive character.[19] He had,
of course, the *au courant* megapolitan feistiness and intellectual
aggression. As with his generation of college-educated and
secularized New York Jewish intellectuals,[20] he felt a mission
of critical enlightenment for the uptight gentiles, though he
often played the ideologue as antiideologue. Odd-man in, he was
much concerned with New York intellectual politics. (He irrele-
vantly complained of his rejection, after earlier acceptance, by
the editors of *Partisan Review,* who treated him better than his
writing merited. Yet an ex-editor, Dwight MacDonald, and his
Politics, provided much of his early reputation as a libertarian
social critic.)[21] He felt rejected by the New York literary and
publishing establishment, yet usually managed to publish beyond
his deserts and was considerably its product. His popular reputation was made by a Jewish magazine and its obtusely manipulative edior (*Commentary,* whose Norman Podhoretz also helped
get Goodman's books published).[22] It was in large part writers
of that milieu who publicly propounded, and perhaps exaggerated, Goodman's importance—though, of course, as fashions
changed they turned on him.[23] While controlled by neither anything as simple as a single coterie nor a clear movement, the
New York Jewish intellectual scene was what Goodman lived
in, and on, and it accounted for much of his publishing access
and public success. It may also account for some of his patent
limitations, from the anxious self-aggrandizement and self-pity
to the distance from mainstream American sensibility and the
consequent pressured position-taking.

As was common to that ambience, what Paul Goodman produced was not fine writing or original thinking but lively intellectual role-playing. Goodman's busy thinking and writing were
less creative than reactive to the local vanguardist and marginal
as well as conventional ideologizing. While the contentious idea-
mongering in such a scene may be limiting and some of the
personal qualities it encouraged may not be very admirable, its
effects may be useful in creating an intellectual culture, or the
simulation of one. It produces not art and wisdom so much as

intellectual games. Intensely and earnestly, Goodman lived that literary life and made its intellectual gestures in a less inhibited way than most. If the limitations and failures are terribly evident, so may be the result—less literature and ideas than the suggestive role, the dissident Man of Letters, the American as literary radical.

II   *The Literary Criticism*

Perhaps the most usual defining activity of the Man of Letters, especially as twentieth-century American intellectual, is that of *belles lettres*, or what has generally been professionalized into "literary criticism." Both designations are unfortunate since *belles lettres* suggests pretty appreciation and other genteel vices, and "criticism" covers altogether too much, from reviewing through textual technology, from petty pedagogy through grand cultural theorizing. Yet some activities between these constitute intelligent discussion of and around literature and become part of literature. If not *the* model for humane discourse in the past century or so, literary criticism had provided many of the modes for it—not only Arnold but Nietzsche, not just the finicky moral discriminations of Leavis within a text but the obsessive ontological elaborations of Sartre on a text, not just the ironic textual patterns of New Criticism but the scientistic analogical labyrinths of French Structuralism. Whether symbolist or psychoanalytic, neo-Aristotelian or neo-Erasmanian, the practice of critical literary dialectics has often been defining of the ways of modern humanistic intelligence. It may still continue so, in spite of the academic-bureaucratic degradation of the critical vocation.[24]

Paul Goodman developed out of this vocation. One of his earliest serious publications was an exercise in the academic *Journal of Philosophy* (March 1934): "Neo-Classicism, Platonism, and Romanticism." Probably written at the age of twenty-two or twenty-three, while he was informally auditing a course at Columbia with a neo-Aristotelian philosopher, Richard McKeon,[25] it is a precocious exercise in aesthetic argument which posits neoclassical rules as equal alternative to neo-Platonic ideas of beauty, and makes some lateral dips into extreme contextualism. The learning, from Longinus to Trotsky, is ranging, sophisticated, and rather ostentatious. The organization is shaky—paragraphs are numbered to partly cover it; the compacted writing wavers between the pedantic and the over-assertive; the argument declares more than it achieves. These were all to become recurrent characteristics of Goodman's writings.

Goodman eventually went on to graduate study in philosophy and literature at the University of Chicago (McKeon had become a dean) while part-time teaching humanities until his dismissal three years later (he reported) for too-public homosexual activity.[26] His doctoral dissertation, finally completed when he was in his forties and published as *The Structure of Literature* (1954)—twenty years after the youthful article which raised its essential points—is an academic exercise of considerable learning and narrow provenance. While claiming to be "inductive formal analysis," *Structure* mostly provides earnest genre application of the stock neo-Aristotelian abstractions. Thus "plot" is defined as a "structure of parts continuous from the beginning to the ending" (p. 274), and in a chapter on "Serious Plots" we find some abstracted cataloguing of elements in *Oedipus, Philoctetes, Richard II*, and, more briefly, some standard epics. A few points are suggestive, such as that the difference between the "tragic" and the "epic" hero is that the first involves character change while the second involves character as fixed in "some habitual virtue" (p. 68). But, as usual in this school, the definitions are covert abstract metaphors and hard-pushed (thus the imagery in *Richard II* becomes part of the "plot") and circular (thus the "experience of *Philoctetes* goes from the beginning to the end and looses tears; it must have some structure or other" [p. 50], i.e., a "serious plot," i.e., a tragic meaning). The neo-Aristotelianism entraps in other ways, too, as in the chapter on "Comic Plots," where Goodman seems to perceive that the comedy of Falstaff undercuts the vicious historical forms and values of *Henry IV, Pt. 1*, but, given the categories (and, apparently, the unacknowledged impress of E. M. Tillyard's conservative interpretation), he can only parenthetically comment on the "contemptible" values implicit in Prince Hal or "digress again" on the play's thinning badly without Falstaff (pp. 111–12).[27] A method, I would say, which either ignores or makes digressive one's most pointed and intense perceptions is quite inadequate.

While the method has some critical utility on neoclassical works, as with formal summaries of Jonson's *Alchemist* and Dryden's *Mac Flecknoe*—though the best points, such as Jonson's anal meanness and Dryden's rhetorical cleverness, are outside the method—the formalism mostly comes a cropper elsewhere. So with the chapter on "Novelistic Plots," which is eccentrically further weakened by taking such thin work as Flaubert's *L'Education sentimentale,* such inappropriate work as *Hamlet,* and by reprinting his own earlier chapter on Kafka's *The Castle.* To demonstrate unintentionally that neo-Aristotelianism has nothing to say about the modern novel, the novel is defined as "an imitation of sentiment" (p. 274). But perhaps aware that something is seriously wrong with the method, the critic repeatedly admits that he is not really analyzing the work "but merely looking abstractly at its structures without inquiring what any of it means" (p. 172). To compensate for such schematic denaturing, meaning burbles back in as vaporized generality—"love, art, and power, and instinctual disgust and disgust in the world, and death—these constitute the magnitude of Hamlet" (p. 172).

A chapter on "Lyrical Poems: Speech, Feeling, Motion of Thought" mostly does a heavily stock metrical analysis of a Catullus poem, a Milton sonnet, and the flabbier sort of Tennyson, which is formalism with a trivial vengeance. (His passing comments on the cool superiority of Catullus or the heroism of Milton are, again, outside the method.) The concluding chapter, "Special Problems of Unity," patches together comments on a mediocre translation by George Dillon of Baudelaire's *"La Géante,"* a few points on a bad poem of Longfellow's (explained as a failure of character), some notes on enlarged allegory in Hawthorne's "The Minister's Black Veil" (whose portentousness Goodman thinks rather too well of); it also rather abstractly considers one of the minor movies of René Clair, and concludes by trying to find the structural correlative of the vicious morality of Corneille's chauvinistic *Horace.* The ostentatious variety of subject hardly overcomes the critical narrowness, and much neo-Aristotelian chatter about beginning-middle-end only underlines *The Structure of Literature*'s own lack of development as it wanders among pedantic commonplaces.

The dubious taste in selections, the total inadequacy with the modern novel, and the aggressive pedantry perhaps as much reflect some academic traditions of several generations ago as they do the limitations of the author, who after all is mostly doing an academic exercise. But most defeating is the literary neutralizing by presuming a "formal structure" separable from and somehow prior to meaning and to the rest of the humane literary experience. With this method, sadly wrong judgments turn into abstracted schematisms which are not correctable because the fuller experience has been obscured in the pseudo-objectification of "form" and "structure." Tragedy and comedy, like plot and character, tend to become emptied devices. Such academic neoclassicism is not just dullingly narrow but critically falsifying.

While Goodman always after carried some of the neo-Aristotelian mannerisms and tastes, his other literary criticism pulled in different directions, including psychoanalytic readings, social-moralistic polemic, and apologies for his own poetry. Though no doubt earnest in his four or so volumes of critical essayings, there is a sense of unseriousness in his subordination of critical response to academic exercise, psychotherapy, social dissent and literary role-playing.

Somewhat more interesting than *The Structure of Literature* and its pedantic formalisms is the more personal and puzzled *Kafka's Prayer*.[28] Now and then this has some of the appeal of, say, Blake's annotations: "Kafka is floundering," he makes "a fatal error," "he says falsely"; near the end Goodman admits, "I began this little book . . . in hatred and envy of Franz . . . more than ready to contradict him. But . . . I have come to love him—the dog" (pp. 250–51); for the book served as "a kind of polemic and self-defense" (p. xii). This sense of fighting with the subject allowed some personal response denied in the pretenses of neo-Aristotelian scientism.

Goodman, reasonably enough, views Kafka as a "sick consciousness," with his literature as willful prayer from a state "near to psychosis" (p. 44) in self-punishing fears. Yet, he argues, slipping through Kafka's anxious strategies or around his self-built barriers to life and happiness were moments of the release of "natural powers" (p. 17) and "natural morality" (p. 47). Thus we can find something exemplary in Kafka's pathetic "infinite regresses" (p. 86) of art and his acrobatic agnosticism. Desperate "within the prison of himself," he "worked by prayerful writing toward our general freedom" (p. 142). The fables, therefore, should be read as an anxious "process" (p. 198) of self-release, of attempting to outwit consciousness and repression and false spiritualization, in order to escape from his own "lamentable character" (p. 207) into life.

This fragmentary, and rather inverted, argument for a natural theology in Kafka insists that he was talking about the self rather than, say, the world of godless bureaucracy. But much of Goodman's supporting psycho-theologizing seems as arbitrary as neo-Aristotelian abstractions. Kafka's pathology around his father and marriage are, of course, undeniable. But Goodman's rather literalist deductions—young Franz witnessing the "primal scene" and "masturbating and withholding orgasm" (p. 31); or the slopped-out psychoanalytic symbolism of persons, hats, swords, and so on as various conditions of the penis (pp. 160 ff.)—don't seem very useful or interesting. As usual with such readings, they short-circuit interpretation into a larger obtuseness. While we can grant that *The Trial* is a "paranoiac dream," to reduce it only to one of "repressed homosexuality" (p. 142) is both too confining and an overextension of a case study of Freud's. Even worse is to see "The Burrow" as the mother's body and the threat as the father's intruding penis (pp. 225–27) because it uses overspecific Freudian ingenuity to miss the main point of the story, which is that the awful "enemy" is the security-seeking self.

While Goodman is a few times suggestive in his antagonistic struggle with Kafka's allegorization of his psychosis, the clinical reductions are tiresome, the treatment is erratic, and the writing is ragged (quite inferior to, say, Gunther Anders or Erich Heller on Kafka.)

But since Goodman was determined to play the critic role and had some publishing "connections," he did pieces on and around literature in a considerable variety of periodicals, including some more notable ones of the time. Because of his peculiarity, he seems to have had a reputation as a vanguardist. Yet, early and late he came out strongly as an eccentric defender of traditionalism. In a sketchy essay written in the early 1940s, "Western

Tradition and World Concern," he laments the loss of culture and the "self-conscious expression of fundamental stories" and suggests that modernist "abstraction is traditional," as with *Finnegans Wake*, in going back to such sources. His condescending criticism of dissident writings of a generation later, such as those by Ginsberg and Kerouac, is for their lack of traditionalism.[29] When he does the rare practical criticism of a text, it is usually a tiredly conventional example, a Milton or Wordsworth anthology piece,[30] or, in one of his most ambitious essays in criticism—"Some Problems of Interpretation: Silence, and Speech as Action"—the main example is the Book of Job.[31] Here, in spite of a speculative hand (and a psychoanalytic finger), Goodman's interpretation is piously conservative, downright scribal. He takes several trivial details as indicating that Job has an "obsessional" neurosis, and therefore his righteousness is compulsive. Job's sick defenses are broken down by Elihu's emotions, and so Job repents, which is confirmed by the deity in the whirlwind. Goodman totally ignores the more interesting modern interpretations in which Job is seen as right as well as righteous in making the existential demand for the deity to justify his unjust order.

The Job critique does not well support Goodman's more interesting argument around it, such as "bearing in mind the nature of speech, it is necessary, in order to interpret a text, to go beyond the text" (p. 238) in "man-to-man encounter . . . and risking one's own logic in the interpretation," a process "indispensable for humanism" (p. 246). This admirable rejection of critical neutrality—literary scientism—is linked to literature as more than mere verbal behavior. Speech is part of rich human action. Goodman emphasizes the genetic: "moral propositions . . . truth or falsity cannot be dissociated from *how* they are held by the man" (p. 247). But here he carries this beyond the psychotherapeutic to an apologia for literature in which the expressed feelings have cognitive as well as emotive value because the "complex words" of literary works "are more adequate observations and hypotheses of reality than any formulas and samplings of psychologists and sociologists" (p. 253). Though emphatically influenced here by New Criticism, it has been turned to posit the Man of Letters as the true social critic.

Influential New Critic John Crowe Ransom, with that tolerance for the eccentric sometimes better found in "conservative" than in "liberal" editors, published a number of Goodman's pieces in the *Kenyon Review*. One of the more ambitious but weird was "Advance-Guard Writing in America: 1900–1950." This does the strange job of never mentioning a single American writer (except for fatuous insults, in passing, at Hemingway and West). He does loosely discuss the homosexual fantasy writers Genet and Cocteau, though they have little significance for his ostensible subject of American writing. Because of personal obsession, he quite overrates them. The lack of other writers may partly be ignorance since the overall evidence suggests that Goodman's literary reading was, after his old-fashioned graduate work, well remembered but often cursory and erratic. Is the ignoring of American writing also spiteful? No doubt, since in his voluminous writings he can hardly ever mention a contemporary (a competitor) other than grudgingly or scornfully. Also: after Cocteau and Genet, he mentions, anonymously, a third sort of vanguardist who writes "occasional poetry," is concerned with community, is not sufficiently appreciated, and so on— his usual self-pitying self-encomium.

The half-accurate generalized history and psychological speculations on how vanguardists may arouse their audience get submerged in such pathetic foolishness. "Good Interim Writing: 1954" and "Underground Writing: 1960" make similar irresponsible gestures, from ignorant cracks about Beat writings to another fatuous dismissal of Nathanael West to praising his own crude fictions. Now and again in such essays there is a touching contextless reflection, such as "one might also say the chief aim of art is to heighten the everyday, to bathe the world in such a light of imagination and criticism that the persons who are living in it without meaning or feeling find that it is meaningful and feelingful to live." Sentimentality is the other side of resentment. Interesting criticism must go beyond such peculiarity.

III *The Literary Criticism of Society*

Goodman partly did go beyond his failure in *belles lettres* by turning literary to social criticism. To turn to his last book around literature, *Speaking and Language* (1971), is to see

several odd strategies. For one, he does not confront other contemporary ideas of literature but takes on a specialist science
with which he is acquainted but hardly expert: modern linguistics (Whorf, Jesperson, Chomsky, and so on). *Speaking* does not
provide an introduction because it shows no mastery of linguistics;
it also does not provide a full countering because it is digressive
to other concerns; but it also does not very fully respond to
literature because it focuses around linguistics. Still, in its ragged
capriciousness it is sometimes suggestive. The fractured development was usual with Goodman, as was the awkward writing,
the clichés, the hoary slang (scram, blab, baloney), and the
rest of what had become compulsive mannerism.[32]

Personal idiosyncracy also would seem to lead to the criticism
of Carnap's *passé* positivism (Goodman had been a student of
his more than thirty years before) and the lengthy arguments
against formal "correctness" in speech and writing. This later
tirade, commonplace to English teachers for a generation before
he wrote, seems motivated as apologetics for his unzippered
pedantry and other eccentricities of verbal dress. Yet scientistic
approaches to language may provide appropriate enemies for
humanistic concern, and *belles lettres* counters to social science.
For those scientizers mostly miss the point: the "structural
linguists disregard the influence of meaning, which is what the
speakers are after"; communications theorists "leave out the
speakers and hearers," the real shapers of the communication;
language positivists and other behaviorists reductively disregard
"variation and invention," which every literary man knows is
crucial; anthropologists of language fail to allow for crossing
cultural boundaries and for change (p. 225). Thus social
scientists not only characteristically misuse language but thoroughly misconstrue it as an impersonal system or "code." Their
idolatrous scientism insists that they do so: "specialist science
and its value-neutral language are an avoidance of experience,
a narrow limitation of the self, and an act of bad faith" (p. 233).
Linguistic and other social scientisms reify language away from
people and their concrete situations, with mechanistic bias (Skinner's behaviorism) or mentalistic bias (Chomsky's Cartesianism), which denies the centrality of the act of speaking, the
situation of dialogue. Goodman holds to a rather Buberian sense

of communion: after all, "it is not minds that communicate, but people. The use of words is itself a creative act, somewhat physical, that produces meaning that did *not* exist in prior thought. People are more changed by changing their pattern of words than their thoughts. Good speech, colloquial or literary, is more meaningful than thought, not less, because it is part of a richer human situation, the dialogue of persons" (p. 221). In this good counterdefining of language, Goodman insists on its communal purposiveness, since "people must explain themselves and have company" (p. 11). Those exigencies, not codes or structures, are what truly speaking is about.

Linguistics is not only wrong for misdefining its subject and for pretentious methodology—"it is impossible for *any* behavioral science to be as precise as scientific linguistics pretends" (p. 91)—but more broadly wrong for subordination to antihumanistic theories. Consequently, linguists fail to recognize that poetry and other literature are "the indispensable renovators of desiccated and corrupted language" (p. 55). To understand language, we need artful attention to specific speaking events. And when it comes to effective speech, there is "no linguistic rule, only moral virtue and literary judgment" (p. 121). The social sciences cannot deal with this, since "it is more important to understand unique cases than to discover general laws" (p. 146). Language, then, is an issue of active culture and style.[33]

We need not push the irony of Goodman's defending literary style against scientism. (He had admitted the year before: "I have written some really hideous paragraphs of sociological and psychological jargon," though he hastily rationalized it "as a kind of shorthand" due to the lack of a "continuing community of readers.")[34] But other matters of style than bad writing also weaken a partly persuasive apologia for the humanistic. After overgeneralizing the modernist claim that "poetry starts from good colloquial speech" (p. 152), he asserts, without any evidence, that "traditional verse forms that have had a great history usually have a basis in nature" (p. 154). But the sheer conventionality of verse forms and their frequent inapplicability to colloquial speech are two of the clearest lessons of modernist poetics. Goodman is, of course, unthinkingly justifying his own traditionalist-imitation versifying; he repeatedly confuses the way he writes with all poetry (pp. 158 ff.). Ironically, the assumption of inherent poetic forms has similarities to Chomsky's argument for inherent linguistic structures, which he is attacking. But Goodman isn't seriously engaging such problems.

Goodman's literary views also suffer from what he accuses the linguists of—lack of the specific.[35] Consequence in point: he says he writes poetry "for no particular audience" (p. 163)— elsewhere he repeatedly claims the opposite ("occasional poetry")—and assumes such alienation to be generally true, though most writers had, and have, specific audiences. Any sophisticated reader must also reject such vulgar overgeneralizations as the smug claims that Men of Letters generally have special "virtues" such as honesty, dedication to love of freedom, and the like, (p. 164). Not tied to specific writers, this is just silly. A better case could easily be made for chameleon duplicity, "negative capability," neurotic ambivalence, sychophancy, and the like, as characteristic of many litterateurs. But Goodman is just naively justifying his own role-playing of the Man of Letters as moral and social prophet. Rather better here is the undeveloped suggestion that "the process of literature is inherent in the nature of language" (p. 165) and therefore is a valid, a knowing, mode in itself.

Playing the literary critic of social forms, Goodman makes some useful points in repeating an old argument of his in the chapter "Format and 'Communications'" (pp. 200 ff.), whose theme is that "format," the imposition of the extrinsic pattern and process, breaks the spirit of writing, destroys essential qualities of the "inherently spontaneous and original." The control-by-format takes various forms under the aegis of the schools, commerce, the exploitative mass media, and the State. As any earnest person who has dealt with most such media soon learns—and by this time Goodman had appeared in many media formats—their processing systematically defeats "the will to *say* anything." He also summarily repeats his educational perception that "school teaching destroys more genuine literacy than it produces," for "school style" exists mostly to serve institutional formulas of control. Surely Goodman is right that the pervasive processing of speech in our culture limits when it doesn't destroy quality. He also aptly notes that subculture formats are limiting and corrupting. Thus the "youth culture" of adolescents quickly succumbs to format processing, and "radical" agitprop—he is responding to the protest movement at the start of the 1970s—can be just as manipulatively jargonized and canned as the officially controlled formats. The processed culture, and its debasement of true speech, is all-pervasive in America, and the Man of Letters should tell us so.

Yet, as so often, Goodman's suggestive views become partly Pyrrhic in context—undercut by ill-considered arguments and marred by personal obsessions. For example, he asserts that "in the end the State is bound together by simple fright, not brainwashing" (p. 203). But even if in the last resort the monopoly of coercion must be used to maintain the State, his own emphasis on controlling "format" points the other way. For the most controlling regimes—Nazi and Stalinist and Maoist—have also been most concerned with dominating formats of expression. Coercion alone is essentially unstable, undependable. (Thus Zamiatin's *We*, which fuses coercion with control of sensibility, seems more insightful than *1984* and *Brave New World*.) Ridden with fearful anxieties, Goodman too readily saw the State as simply coercing the "natural" instead of attempting to transform or replace it.

With this goes a Rousseauean theology, a dualism of institutional evil versus the "natural." Here Goodman wanted to find the good "natural" in uninstitutionalized speech: "colloquial speech is quite impervious to corruption by format" (p. 206); "people who can talk can be oppressed but not brainwashed." Would that this circular definition of "good colloquial" freedom were adequate. Obviously behavior, which includes speech (as he has argued against the linguists), is often corruptible and corrupted by the schools, media, and other institutions. For that very reason, Goodman was to spend much of his life arguing for their decentralization, depowering, or downright abolition.

Goodman, then, is more suggestive than adequate, more earnest than serious, in failing to follow through very well on the lineaments and limitations of his own arguments for the Man of Letters as critical custodian of free consciousness.[36] In his last book of social criticism as such, *New Reformation*, he speaks of his role of "social critic" as a humanistic and literary one, partly in the manner of the Enlightenment Man of Letters (pp. 113–18).[37] For literary engagement itself is a deep expression of natural powers: "Literature is both too complicated and too free wheeling to be followed without spontaneous attention springing from desire" (p. 116). Setting aside the bad overgeneralization of this to all literature, indiscriminately, it may be true that certain literary traditions (Western, modern, individualistic, rebellious) have produced "habits, genres, and tropes" which "constitute a method of coping with reality different from science, political power, or common sense." While "literature is a method *sui generis*," it is also "a part of philosophy" in the broad sense. In its peculiar combination of shaping and remembering, desire and observation, and human events of dialogue, literary understanding becomes "the warrant by which a man of letters can be a social critic" (p. 114).

While the argument grossly lacks discrimination and development—surely much of what is called literature contains no such warrants; certainly there is more than one kind of warrant—we can see his purpose. While Goodman, as I hope I have fairly indicated, didn't do much good literary criticism in his nearly forty years of intermittent practice of it, he did find some sanctions by which the literary critic was the humanistic social critic *par excellence*.[38] Granted that literature can be a true mode of understanding, its critical edges may be turned against society, and with rather more pertinence than can be mustered by those with mere political knowledge, or social and psychological scientism, or even our ordinary sense of social reality. The literary man may delegislate the unacknowledging world. The true Man of Letters is the proper libertarian.

CHAPTER 2

The Conservative Anarchist

I Working Anarchism

IN his thirties Paul Goodman began to identify his version of
the literary-radical role as "anarchism." Without questioning his
sincerity, his position served as a black-flagging that truly one-
bettered his mostly Marxist-colored or liberal-toned New York
intellectual peers. It gave Goodman a distinctive place as probably
the best-known literary anarchist in America, and *the* public
one in the 1960s. But in several ways it is odd that Goodman
became an avowed anarchist in the mid-1940s. He showed little
interest in libertarianism, or even in much of what was then
called "social conscience," in his student days, in his twenties,
and in most of his writings.[1] He was not in most usual senses
a rebellious character as a student—far less one than most who
became anarchists. His anxious and defensive self-conceit, his
petty bourgeois origins, his narrow worldly experience and con-
finement to a New York *lumpen*-intellectual milieu, his insistent
role-playing as Artist and Man of Letters, his lack of concern
with most issues of equality and justice—these hardly encourage
the styles of the great rebel or revolutionary. Incidental remarks
suggest that Goodman feared and disdained those types, too.
Yet he was a rebel in some of his writings and public roles, if
not in spite of himself at least because of an odd "spite," as he
several times acknowledged. He parenthetically comments in
The Empire City (p. 546) that "the way I exercise my spite is
to depict the good community possible to reasonable people but
not possible to you." Behind this, no doubt, were other resentments.

The dreams of a "good community," where he would have more
acceptance and place, become dominant in his thought. Anarchists are necessarily utopians, in part and in varied ways,

37

because their demands on the social order so outdistance the realities. At least since the classical Cynics, the original libertarian rebels in Western tradition, propounded the free and easy Island of Para, the anarchist-minded have yearned after utopia, or as Goodman more often put it, practiced "millenarian hopes." Part of Goodman's libertarian motive was an intellectual as well as personal despair: "I invented a different and practical world than this world that made no sense and took the heart out of me."[2]

Goodman's anarchism also displays other impetuses than the reactive resentments and despairs—other aesthetic ones. Probably the most likely social ideology for the artistic avant-garde has been some version of libertarianism. After all, anarchism is the most imaginative of political views, given usual politics. Goodman's main young rebelliousness, other than his bisexuality, was to conceive of himself as an Artist, and the ambience, including the marginality and failure, was vanguardist. As a heritage of the nineteenth century, anarchism was to politics what vanguardism was to culture, not least in the often eccentric and extreme tone as well as in the defiant and experimental (including the sexual) freedom for the exceptional.[3]

Goodman arrived at anarchism during World War II. His rejection of the draft, which he avoided, and his revulsion at the cultural and social conditions of wartime, which he saw as ugly, may have provided some of the specific occasion for his first anarchist essays in 1945. The publishing possibilities in several libertarian journals—*Politics, Why?, Retort*—provided places for him as a dissident writer. Apparently, his associations in that period with some anarchopacifists provided much of his libertarian ideas and language.[4] His bohemianism sanctioned anarchism—and vice versa. Anarchism provided literary and social roles for a faltering and aging writer. It is no denigration or charge of insincerity to suggest that one might choose libertarian politics the way one chooses a genre or an aesthetic manner. Anarchism can be a high style. Goodman combined his apprentice anarchist essays with literary essays in *Art and Social Nature* because for him society was in considerable part an aesthetic issue, both personally as a faltering vanguard artist and in larger social vision.

Indeed, "inventiveness"—similar to what would later be meant by the cant term "creativity"—plays a key role in several of the early anarchist essays. As he rhetorically concludes the six collectively subtitled "The May Pamphlet,"[5] libertarianism is the effort to release "natural powers" and create a "free history" such as one finds in "poems, heroic and saintly deeds" and others which "have a difference and inventiveness" (p. 45). We invent, socially as well as artistically, by releasing nature, and this, as most writers tend to feel, is less by outburst than accretion. As the first essay opens: "A free society cannot be the substitution of a 'new order' for the old order; it is the extension of spheres of free action until they make up most of the social life" (p. 2). While he parenthetically counters the reformist tone of this by adding that "any genuine liberation whatsoever involves a total change," he always had a conserving distaste for revolutionary proposals and styles, consciously at least. His enduring slogan: "*Free action is to live in present society as though it were a natural society*" (p. 3).[6]

The difficulties here may be in what constitutes the "natural" and what qualifies as "free" living. But for Goodman, social mutuality is "natural" and freedom is to do those actions "which clash openly with the coercive laws," defined as that which "*prevents a human power from becoming a living act*" (pp. 3–4). A specific is "the modern industrial system" with its time-restraints, division of labor, and other controls, though unemployed Goodman doesn't quite say one should refuse to work. Another is the overt sexuality of children, of which "*even lack of encouragement*" is "unnatural coercion" (p. 6). In 1945 that appeared outrageous to the often puritanic leftists.

This essay, entitled "Reflections on Drawing the Line"—the limits beyond which a libertarian would resist—is in fact a rejection of any such imprudently defiant course (and apparently of some of the anarcho-pacifists he knew), except for non-allegiance to the system generally, and sexual repression: "A free man . . . would not have finally to draw a line in their absurd conditions . . ." (p. 10). He would merely live his sexually polymorphous bohemian-artist life. As did Goodman.

The second brief essay turns somewhat more ambiguously to the personal-therapeutic benefits that might result from an "apparently trivial" (p. 16) act of resistance. The third essay, "A Touchstone for the Libertarian Program," seems to make a drastic advocacy of *"a large number of precisely those acts and words for which persons are in fact thrown into jail"* (p. 18). But it doesn't really, since the purpose is just therapeutic: "What I urge is not that the libertarian bestir himself to commit such 'crimes'—I don't think, by the way, that our small numbers would inconveniently crowd the jails—but that he at once loosen his own 'discipline' and prejudice against these acts" (p. 19). For "our acts of liberty are our strongest propaganda." By this he apparently means unconventional *personal* behavior, the sexually and socially marginal, done with some public prudence. Goodman's psychology fails to recognize that the personal break with prevailing social norms often requires cathartic defiance, political excess, a more extreme style—as the history of radicalism, and radicals, insistently confirms.[7]

While Goodman's vague and circular standards, such as "the natural behavior of natural groups" (p. 20), don't tell us much, the fourth brief essay, "Natural Violence," does point to a modern problem. The "sterilization" of "primary experiences" (birth, sex, death) in our urban society leads to the denial of the "natural" and therefore to the need to turn to displaced aggressions. "War is unnatural violence" (p. 24), which cannot have a healing Rousseauistic and Taoistic acceptance.

The remaining two essays in his early libertarian pamphlet show somewhat more theoretical reach. "Revolution, Sociolatry, and War" originally appeared in Dwight MacDonald's *Politics* and, as was pretty much the mandated style there, works out its ex-Marxist editor's libertarian revulsions to Marx. Goodman praises Marx's social psychology but finds him historically wrong in such postulates as "the iron law of wages" (actually, this was the revisionists' version of the historical necessity in capitalism of "the pauperization of the proletariat"). Marxism is "bankrupt" and "reactionary" (p. 30) in its statism and other politics. Goodman's counterpolitics depends on arousing "natural powers," that he optimistically sees as "immeasurably stronger" than "alien institutions" which are only "pale sublimations." This, again, is to be promoted by "small group" accretions of fraternal freedom, and opposition to the social-idolatry of sublimating our deeper nature in the usual socioeconomic goals. The alternative aims are neither American nor Marxist, "not the efficient production of commodities, but cooperative jobs themselves worth doing" (p. 31). This requires what European libertarians call Worker's Control, as well as the sexual liberation of the young, the rejection of representative majoritarianism and bureaucracy for decentralism and direct political initiative, and of course abstention from all connected with the war (pp. 31–33). This sketchy program is conventional anarchism, except for the application of psychoanalytic notions of repression, sex and aggression.[8] From the late Freud, Goodman accepts the inevitability of some aggression, to be "moderated by small-scale fraternal competition, mutual aid, and instinctual gratification" (p. 33), which are to be the invention of "natural institutions."[9]

The concluding essay, "Unanimity," suggestively follows this with the argument that "natural conflict is solved only by invention" (p. 36) of social alternatives. Reformist actions, such as democratizing the military (an issue discussed at that time in *Politics*) or conventional defenses of civil liberties, are rejected for a more radical attack on the "social dilemmas" (p. 37). And here we get that positive thinking (I take it to be a peculiarly American vice) that was to be obsessive in his social criticisms, perhaps to allay his anxious hostilities. He makes, I think, the false claim that "negative criticism insults and disheartens" (p. 37), taking no account of possibilities of purging and enlivening and opening. "If a man cannot invent a way out, what right has such a man to be a libertarian on the issue at all?"

But the libertarian will not accept the "lesser evil"; instead, he must look for the creative possibility that will reach the psychoanalytically "deeper" levels. Goodman presupposes an "unchanging human nature" (p. 44), a fraternal wisdom larger than that of the individual, and social-political agreement as something of a therapeutic process. What may be most interesting here is the restatement of the anarchist insistence on "unanimity" rather than "representation" and "majority rule." The latter, of course, do not give either real individual or group choice and provide a falsely uncoercive coloration to the choices of a few, often within imposed alternatives.[10] Increased numbers also patently do not provide increased wisdom. Frequently, "tossing

a coin" would give as much "just decision" (p. 40). Revealingly,
in the intercourse of friends we almost never decide by majority
vote but either work to a general agreement or accede to the
choice of the most concerned person. And Goodman argues that
"for the most part unanimity is not found by relaxing but by
sharpening the conflict, without unnatural coercion, until the
emergence of a new idea" (p. 39). Only thus will we get "social
initiative" and the release of the positive.[11]

This anarchism of the literary intellectual, with its rather
Blakean contraries, stays, as Goodman notes, within the "essence
of libertarian thought, except to add to it some notions of the
psychoanalysis" (p. 42). That social psychology, and the decentralizing, the liberating of the young, the peace politics, were to
continue to occupy him. But theoretic concepts such as unanimity
were to be largely displaced by topical issues such as education.
His twenty-odd years of social criticism were to be more on the
side of application than theory, less inventing anarchism than
its cases. But Goodman had invented for himself some new
literary roles and work. Sometimes his anarchism was just a
simple pious formula, such as "if we undo the State and relax
the repression of children, then the good society will flourish."[12]
But he was also sometimes to see more perplexing issues of social
liberation.

II   Communitas

Undoubtedly one of Paul Goodman's most seminal essays, and
probably still his best book, is *Communitas*, subtitled "Means
of Livelihood and Ways of Life."[13] Though some of the material
now seems a bit dated (originally published in 1947, it was
revised for a new edition in 1960), it remains suggestive not
only on urban planning issues but of ways of utopian social
thinking. If it weren't such a contradiction in terms, one might
call this "imaginative sociology" for its unusual combination of
speculative moral philosophy and concrete social problem. It is
not utopian in the mad fantasy, the merely projective, sense.
The need for "human scale" (p. 222) in our thinking about our
buildings and our cities, and more generally in our economics
and our social orderings, provides the basic theme of the essay.

In part, *Communitas* is laid out as an illustrated (by coauthor-brother Percival Goodman) primer for teaching some of the implications of existing city plans, and hence social-economic orderings, and to raise possibilities of making "positive decisions for one's communty" since that "is one of the noble acts of man" (p. 11). It might be viewed as some libertarian footnotes to Plato's *Republic*. The Goodmans often display a nice critical edge against conventional responses, such as the not recognizing "there are alternative choices" (p. 12) to most of our communal arrangements. We have been imposed upon by certain fashions in false necessity, such as that it "is more efficient to centralize, whereas it is usually more inefficient" (p. 13), and by "the absurdity of the American Standard of Living" (p. 14). Much of the Goodman standard here is rather un-American, even for radical social criticism, in being less concerned with *justice* than with the *social aesthetic*—"beauty is our criterion" (p. 17).

Approximately the first half of the small book consists of sketches of some modern views of urban possibilities: the greening by Garden Cities, and the like (Geddes, Howard, Unwin, etc.); the economic rationalization of urban production in essentially Industrial Plans (an historic American mill town, some Soviet and Chinese mammoth industrial projects, Buckminster Fuller's technocratic utopia, and so on); and Integrated Plans combining urban and rural in a humane scale (TVA, Frank Lloyd Wright, Borsodian home production, the kibbutz, the progressive school). One limitation is the drastic brevity, even if intended as just illustrative and suggestive. Another is the extreme New Yorker prejudices (in the text as well as in the four appendixes devoted to planning possibilities of that miserable city). Thus they assume that most interesting culture belongs to mammoth modern cities; exurbanite life is that of "ignorant, smug parasites" (p. 30); suburban culture and styles are inherently "petty bourgeois" (p. 29); and an "intellectual would rather meet a bear in the woods" (p. 35) than live in a Garden City. This facile identification of certain class cultures with certain layouts of the environment is also unfair to the Garden City concepts. It may merge certain historical part-accidents—the midcentury American petty bourgeois flight to the suburbs—with certain physical plans, which may not always be true. But

it is true that modern suburban ways of life tend schizophren-
ically to separate domesticity from a richer integration with work
and culture, and that is the crux of the problem.

If the application of Garden City ideas produces insufficient
integration of life, this is even more true of the industrially
dominated plans with their narrow technical functionalism. The
Goodmans cast a cool eye on both private capitalist (American)
and state capitalist (Soviet) industrial-city projects, and a harsh
eye on the technopathology of Buckminster Fuller (pp. 76–82).[14]
Along the way, Goodman makes nice points about the lack of
humane aesthetic: so with the "International Style" and Le Corbusier's housing as machines-for-living; thus the need for human
scaled squares for richer life in public; so the gross inefficiency
of our mass movement of people instead of things; thus the outrageous American mania for largeness in industrial buildings and
conurbations and plans (p. 84). These lead to notes on some
various approaches to integration of work and living, of agriculture and manufacturing, of new communal development
(kibbutz) and regional development (TVA). Given the Goodman view, they too briefly comment on "intentional communities"
(pp. 103 ff.). They note with sad irony that such efforts now
seem to require one "to be disgusted with the common way," to
have "a burning ideal to share," and to have the disappearing
humanity of "a cooperative character" (p. 105). Communal attempts, they also suggest, may be similar to vanguardist arts in
that they seem to fail but may pass on certain aspirations to
broader or later efforts. Some communal efforts in the 1960s
may have been influenced by Paul Goodman: several progressive
schools, certain notions of "Free Universities," and possibly even
some of the living-working communes. One might regret that
Goodman didn't return to the subject of communal efforts in his
later writings.[15]

The second half of *Communitas*, "Three Community Paradigms," goes beyond the historical sketches of plans to the
Goodmans' own imaginative proposals, a near-novelistic effort
(and more so than in Goodman's avowed fictions), which seeks
"to give important value choices as if they were alternative
programs" (p. 119). With unusual irony for Paul Goodman, the
first paradigm-plan aims at compulsive consumption—other, that

is, than "such luxury commodities as tanks, bombers," and the like (p. 121)—with the central city as a "Department Store" (pp. 125 ff.), one "immense container" for eliminating selling-buying inefficiency and discomfort (e.g., city streets, separation of living from buying). It is a mocking metaphoric elaboration of the present ordering of our consumer society. The profile properly ends with a Saturnalia, a potlatching festival which cleans out the fetish objects for a new round of consumption. The department-store-city social relations and politics, it is suggested, would be of the same advertiser-consumption-mania style. "An existence of this kind, apparently so repugnant to craftsmen, farmers, artists, or any others who want a say in what they lend their hands to, is nevertheless satisfactory to the mass of our countrymen, so it must express deep and universal impulses" (p. 148).

The second imaginative sketch for a new form of community takes more positive form, within the libertarian traditions of freeing work, developing industrial democracy, and creating integrated communities with aesthetic qualities. It closely relates "the personal and productive," provides political and economic control of industry by the collectivity of "experienced workers," and redesigns labor as well as domestic arrangements on "psychological and moral as well as technical grounds" for the "well-rounded" and diversified development of self-sufficient communities (p. 155). That requires the combination of the urban and rural, and decentralized federalism. Much of this comes from the visions of enlightenment utopians and their continuation by nineteenth-century anarchists, such as Kropotkin, leavened with technologically advanced domestic production (Borsodi), contemporary progressive education (Reich and Neill), morally selected mid-twentieth-century functionalist design (from the romantics through the pragmatists to Wright), and a rather fanciful return to the organic public style of life (Greek and medieval) around communal squares and rituals.[16]

What would be the culture—the arts and festivals and styles and sensibilities—expressing the mythos of such communities? "We don't know" (p. 166). The charm of that undogmatic candor—and of providing illustrations of the nonexistent!—does not quite obscure that such a total reorientation of social life requires some-

thing on the order of a revolutionary-religious movement. Sensitive and sagacious plans for a community, artfully cooperative
instead of competitively power-mad, must draw on deeper and
more perplexed sources than here acknowledged. The Goodmans
present us less with a "vision" of the good life than a prevision of
it; they less provide a utopian vista of the future than some social-
aesthetic criteria for it.

Not surprisingly, then, the Goodmans don't consider the de-
pressing issues of how we might get to such an organic ordering
from our highly bureaucratized and otherwise elaborately arbitrary money and power structure. They provide, instead, a series
of aesthetic notes on such subjects as the lovely simplicity of
traditional Japanese home furnishing and on "The Moral Selection of Machines"—clear utility, repairability by the user, relative
autonomy, and the like. They make a variety of "practical" suggestions, from planting in cities what grows naturally (weeds!),
to purifying home decoration and simplifying nurses' uniforms
and dispersing museum objects throughout the city. Some proposals, such as that business scheduling not be time-clock rigid
but by function and varying individual taste, have had, a generation later, some publicized small applications. The Goodmans, of
course, take swipes at the bad aesthetics of American advertising
and at the "booby trap" values of typical American consumption.
The "home of the average American" maximizes "the worst possible community arrangement" because it imposes on all aspects
of private life impersonal products which lack public values,
since our "only moral aim" is "to provide private satisfactions
called the Standard of Living" (p. 184). American communal
purpose is to be a noncommunity. This results in styles that cannot properly be said to have either public or private large satisfactions. In contrast, they want us to examine our production and
consumption in "neo-functionalist" ways: "Efficient for what? For
the way of life as a whole" (p. 172).[17]

This paradigm of an integrated community with neo-functionalist aesthetics is the positively "utopian, it is the child-heart of
man" (p. 220). Yet with more cynical wariness the Goodmans
sketched two antithetical paradigms: the city as optimally de-
signed department store, which at least has an aesthetic, however
baroque, and some style, however immoral—now partly realized

in some of our grandiloquent shopping centers. And, in contrast to the immoral and the unlikely, a third paradigm presents a disenchanted radicalism. This proposes spartan but stylishly simple communities for part of the society, part of the time, as part of a consciously dual economy—a semiautonomous subsistence economy of decent poverty within the affluently exploitative economy. As the authors are aware, we already had a badly done dual economy with a substantial population on "welfare" and various other forms of subsistence. But the Goodmans' proposal entails a more direct—and less hypocritical (but that is the rub!)—subsistence ordering with its own simple housing, food, services, *and* worthwhile work. They guess that only a small part of economic activity in America (originally a tenth; a fifteenth in the revised edition; now a twentieth?) could reasonably be said to go for basic human needs. By a highly speculative calculus, they come up with a limited period such as seven years for which everyone might be required to serve the subsistence system, and for which they would receive the basic lifelong support. Those who wanted to buy their way out could, and all would be free to switch over to the mad economy of affluence. Within the bounds of a minimal economic style, the tithe of time would provide permanent economic freedom. Here would be autonomy and decency not just for the "disadvantaged" but for the "marginal," those with other values than the usual aggrandizements—a central point since Goodman's arguments frequently turn around his New York bohemian community's needs.

The notion of a subsistence economy within the other goes back through certain European social insurance schemes, such last-century experiments as the workshops of Louis Blanc, and—unacknowledged—the monastic life. Indeed, I think the Goodmans' proposal might be more feasible in form if conceived as secularized monasteries to which victims and dissidents and marginals *could* withdraw for subsistence living with a limited work requirement—a minimal utopia within the dominant system. But though their impetus was a plan to escape from the totalitarian inclusiveness of modern economics, which makes it difficult to be decently poor, they, too, ended up with a coercive system by universalizing the service requirement. Ironically, they rightly saw in "the union of government and economy . . . the full tide

toward statism" (p. 189), inevitable in a system of "inhuman
scale" which must be maintained at foolish and forced activity
simply not to break down. When not expanding in arbitrary ways
beyond any rational criteria for production and needs and humane
desires, our economy degenerates into massive unemployment,
capital collapse, tax deficiency, state intervention, and general
crisis. For the good of society, then, as well as of themselves, a
considerable number should be able to opt out. But the Goodmans'
somewhat militarylike requirement of service in the subsistence
economy for everyone rather Calvinistically violates their own
libertarian temper. Since they wrote, advocates of the "guaranteed annual income," and similar proposals, have also unsuccess-
fully attempted to respond to the issues.[18]

A later comment notes that the subsistence economy paradigm
has a special appropriateness for nonindustrialized areas and
countries, in contrast to the destructive imposition of our lavish
technological ordering (p. 219). The Goodman proposal of a
dual economy is paradoxically conservative, even beyond the
acknowledgment of "the paradox that the wildest anarchists are
generally affirming the most ancient values" of organic order and
dignified community "as if they lived in neolithic times or the
Middle Ages," whereas "the so-called conservatives are generally
arguing for policies and prejudices" of just a generation ago,
conserving little but greed and fear (p. 10). At times their argument suggests that our society cannot be expected to conserve
the rational and humane, or find its way back to human scale as
a whole. Therefore, all that can be done is to provide an escape
route for some, a socioeconomic saving remnant. Subsistence
schemes, such as their third paradigm of community, despair of
sufficient social revolution. Yet they want to see the proposal as
not just palliative, reformist; it would have radical effects because
the American "moral attitude . . . would be profoundly deranged"
(p. 212) by real economic freedom. With alternatives to submission to the "general economy," many would become subjects
for either demagogic fears or new liberations (pp. 213 ff.).
(The "counterculture" of the recent past seems to have confirmed
this.) A palliative double-economic system, then, may be transi-
tional, educational, to social revolution by opening the coerced

to other possibilities, making many newly aware of life outside "the Standard of Living of Americans" (p. 217).

In a nicely sarcastic paragraph, the Goodmans also mention a "fourth attitude toward the economy of abundance ... [which] implies a fourth community scheme"—perhaps the most likely but least interesting of all: endless war production. This not only disposes of surpluses, thus keeping the economy expanding, but also disposes of "the producers and the consumers," a popular dystopianism with "an efficient schedule for returning from the Sixth to before the First day" (p. 221). Such fabulistic irony suggests some of the resonance proper to this libertarian pedagogy for a better, a more humanely limited, sense of community. Yet, of course, Goodmanism tends exaltingly to isolate "community" as a value, separating it from other kinds of freedom as well as privacy, equality, and other values, as the ultimate good, forgetting that there were some good reasons for our fleeing the old communities.[19] However interesting and suggestive, they hardly provide a full libertarian social vision.

III *Decentralizing*

Paul Goodman's *Communitas*, in my view, was and remains his best book. Still, some of its motifs were sometimes interestingly developed in other works. Some years later, in a very brief but cogent summary, "Reflections On the Anarchist Principle" (1966),[20] he capsulates, for an anarchist audience, what he judges almost all anarchists have in common: "Anarchists want to increase intrinsic functioning and diminish extrinsic power" (p. 176). The principle has massive empirical support in that most of our centralized and hierarchical authorities and their coercions do more harm than good. Exceptions might be *temporary* emergencies, *limited* general services (such as pure water), and some relatively *neutral* administering (such as weights and measures), but even those must be watched so that they stay temporary, limited, neutral. In social context, Goodman (as we shall see) makes other considerable exceptions, but the principle should be clear. Which, however, does not mean that its application is always the same. For examples: In relation to royal patents and mercantilist policies, small "free enterprize" with open market autonomy (Adam

Smith) was libertarian in ways it cannot possibly be under vast
corporate structures, mergence with the state, monopolistic conditions, and manipulated markets and consumers. Some constitutional forms—independence of the judiciary, codified rights, increase in protective law—may be liberating at some times but
controlling (by legal cliques) and repressive (of the disadvantaged) at other times. Free universal education, a longtime
anarchist demand in enlightenment faith, has turned into hier-
archically controlling and indoctrinating "School Systems" so that
no seasoned libertarian (in contrast to "liberals") now favors extended compulsory education. Thus there "cannot be a history of
anarchism in the sense of establishing a permanent state of things
called 'anarchist'" (p. 177). Depowering and liberating are not
devices and dogmas but a philosophy.

This historical shiftiness of social forms becomes crucial in
postmodern changes. As Goodman presents a related argument in
an important occasional essay of the same period, "Two Points
of Philosophy and an Example" (1967),[21] he moderates his anarchism (as he was often to do in his later years) to something of a
disenchanted liberalism, for a liberal audience, to emphasize what
has been done in our time by a "change of scale," and its reverse
effects. For example, whatever effects jailing once could claim
(penance, punishment, reform, limiting crime), it now rather
insistently produces mostly opposite effects, including increase
in crime and "*heightening* of social anxiety" (p. 56). The vast
increase in mass schooling now rather more interferes with education, at the level of simple literary as well as more sophisticated
intellectuality, than advances it. A number of advanced and enlarged health policies now generate (as Illich was to more systematically argue in *Medical Nemesis*) ill health, inadequacy, and
death. (Goodman mentions the birth-control pill and hospitaliza-
tion; one could add some immunization programs, such as for
"swine flu" in 1977, pesticide treatments of the environment,
WW II period therapeutic radiology, excessive surgery, medical
dependency, and others.) Similar points can be made about much
of urban and transportation planning, which help destroy the
true amenities of cities, and about massive communications systems, which make it harder to come by truth and sensibility. The
change of scale, rather than evil motives, produces contrary

effects. (Enlarging scale, one suspects, should itself be identified as an evil motive.) And here technology, which Goodman insists is "a branch of moral philosophy" (p. 55), is put to the question, along with "increased population" and our economic and social megalomanias.

Curiously, Goodman sidesteps those—though, of course, the essay is fractured in organization, as usual—to ingeniously apply some diluted anarchism toward keeping society partly open. Since hierarchical planning will continue, we need to control it by "a kind of constitutional limit to planning" (p. 61) and, more importantly, by the development of "countervailing" powers, including guaranteed incomes, dispersal of decisions, and community controls on experts. He also has a hobby-horse to ride: "rural reconstruction" (p. 66) as an answer to overurbanization as well as our new "enclosure" movement of technological and commercial exploitation which drastically drove people off the land and dumped them in miserable conditions in the cities. Goodman suggests several schemes, such as moving welfare cases to welfare-plus-subsistence farming so they would live better, and out of the cities; he also suggests extended boarding in rural regions of urban children.[22] These palliatives lack organic community and ways of life and seem diluted versions of the libertarian principle of fusion of urban and rural. Why this reduction of his own principles? To be "practical," and perhaps appropriate to an essentially liberal audience; but perhaps more importantly, despair. For he doubts that there "can be a significant cutback in urbanization in this generation" (p. 66), even though the cities are desperate. (Since he wrote, there has been some small trend to deurbanization.) This reformist strategy, of using background libertarian principles for suggesting "options in an increasingly monolithic society," dominates much of Goodman's later social criticism.

In his popular role as social critic, Goodman often adapted anarchist philosophy to limited reforms. But the two kinds of decentralizing (pointed to in the two essays discussed), libertarian and palliative, are not always separated out. While his social criticisms in the 1960s often did not well serve the anarchist temper, they may have been striking to less radical audiences. One of his most ambitious essays of this period, *People or Per-*

sonnel, subtitled "Decentralizing and the Mixed System," might reasonably be characterized as libertarianized reformism. But the most cogent charge against the prevailing economic-social order is radical. In a vicious circularity, "people work to keep the economic system in operation and the system operates in order to keep people working" (p. 117). Thus we more and more get a "social machine for its own sake" (p. 137). Certain personnel, of course, do profit from it, such as the feudal overlords of the private and state baronies and the "major new class of bureaucratized intellectuals, a kind of monkhood" (p. 30) of "professionals" who man these structures. They come to largely identify with "the very aggrandizement of the organization" (p. 71) which, because of the lack of "countervailing forces, leads to far-reaching social effects that were not at all intended."

We now have such large and interlocked organizations in industry, government, philanthropy, agriculture, schooling, commerce, media, culture, and science, which show what Goodman calls "the centralizing style." Such systematization has gone so far as to "become ineffectual, economically wasteful, humanly stultifying, and ruinous to democracy" (p. 3). Its characteristics include "top down" authority, "chain of command," "standard performance" (p. 4), "concentration of power" (p. 19) and its aggrandizement, "rigidly set forms and rituals" (p. 60), treatment of people in organizational terms ("personnel"), behavior that is obsessively "abstract and indirect" (p. 89), endless procedural emphasis, extreme internalizing of status considerations (p. 134), and a pervasive sense of "powerlessness for most as persons." It isn't much questioned—all conventional political views, liberal and conservative, "share the belief in top-down management" (p. 29), so "the centralist style exists as a mass superstition" (p. 5) and creates the *anomie* which is our most pervasive social disease.

It is an apt indictment; but strange, from an anarchist point of view, is Goodman's lack of concern about, for example, hierarchy as such, for that can also be found in relatively small organizations. Goodman also does not much object to economic and social inequality. In his support of what he takes to be "pluralism," with variety and "countervailing powers" (p. 137), he defends profit systems when they can be "strictly limited in their power to sabotage excellence and do injustice" (p. 124), though for him injustice is not inequality since "if everybody has enough, it doesn't much matter if some operators get a disproportionate share." This bland allowance of economic inequalities, created by a social system, to unjustly aggrandise or misuse natural inequalities, is not the egalitarianism of anarchism but a confusion of contemporary liberalism.[23] So may be the pragmatic-reformist cast of what he declares to be his theme: the "political *maxim*: to decentralize where, how, and how much is expedient. But where, how, and how much are empirical questions" (p. 27). No, I would say, drawing on Goodman's sometimes-libertarian view, they are philosophical questions, such as what makes the best ways of working and living.

Not accidentally, Goodman starts and concludes *People or Personnel* with positive comments on standard college-student audiences; I suggest his reach was to bring in the somewhat-educated and earnest-liberal middle class. Perhaps such was the price of the available public role. This, of course, does not deny that his ragged discussion develops numerous insights, including criticisms of stock liberalism ("corporate liberalism" militants called it in the 1960s). Much of liberalism aggrandizes centralism through statist palliatives and bureaucratization, especially in "welfare," schooling, unionization, and cultural and political institutionalization. Here "the rhetoric of Liberalism has become paternalistic . . . and promises to lead us right to 1984" (p. 32). City services accelerate the problem. "The increase of urban social disease and urban mental illness is fundamentally due to powerlessness, resignation, and withdrawal, as if people's only way to assert vitality is to develop symptoms" (p. 17). The professional "monks" and their programs tend to increase the illness, the state of being "chronic patients," rather than advancing humane communities. The critic also radically notes that "there is a limit of urban density and urban sprawl beyond which *no* form of organization, centralist or decentralist, can cope" (p. 18).

Large hierarchies, of course, show their weakness in getting true information up a change of command, and good performance requirements down it (pp. 77 ff.), but perhaps more important is their inherent mediocrity in "personnel" handling: "the salient cause of ineptitude in promotion and in all hiring practices is

that under centralized conditions, fewer and fewer know what *is*
a good job of work" (p. 83), and certainly not those in authority.
So, in compensation, these structures develop elaborate systems
which tend to be humanly defeating.[24] All true enough, as anyone
who has spent years in mediocre bureaucracies knows, though
Goodman has little to say about why it came about, except for
the false centralizing (and hierarchical) ideology; he ignores the
advantages of mediocrity for many.

Attacks on bureaucracy often seem to be a "conservative"
gesture. Goodman rightly dismisses this, for the pseudoideological
conflict between business and government just carries on "the
ancient war of the King and the Barons" (p. 30). He critiques
four baronial structures. The New York City school system is
"an example of classical bureaucracy" (p. 50), and one which
can no longer educate. American food growing–processing–dis-
tributing (pp. 66–71) has destroyed quality, the rural ways of
life, and, in spite of being unnecessarily expensive, has destroyed
profits for many farmers and others. The vast transportation system of cars, highways, and the related, is even worse in destroying communal qualities and amenities. Here Goodman feels
driven against his own principles: "In the mess we are in . . . I
can see no remedy but authoritarian public planning to express
further community needs than making profits for automobile
manufacturers" (p. 60). But perhaps Goodman is most apt on the
mass-media systems, which are run by "men who should not
wield cultural power" (p. 66). He repeats the "format" argument (previously discussed) of rigid processing which controls,
and defeats, all, and concludes that the saturation controls see to
it that "none of these [programs] can speak profoundly or finish,
so there is continual stimulation and inadequate discharge, and
therefore compulsion to repeat. As with most of the rest of the
American standard of living, the system flourishes by *preventing*
serious or absorbing satisfaction" (p. 65).

That, to adapt Michels, might be considered an Iron Law of
Bureaucratized Sensibility. And this sense of issue, though sometimes poorly focused by Goodman's rough ("plenty tasteless")
and clichéd writing, and an overemphasis on financial arguments
(and now dated figures and proportions), seems good. So does
the recognition that centralizing order is class biased; not only

do those bureaucratized professionals need subjects—"client-personnel of the professional-personnel" (p. 133)—but they enforce class differences, with the middle class dominating the conformist and paper-ridden command style in which such "mandarinism is most disadvantageous to poor people" (p. 88). Ostensibly protective of the "disadvantaged," the bureaucratic monks would even guide them in their freedom and leisure. But if "people have not been rendered stupid and powerless, by schools and liberals among others, they will no doubt know what to do with themselves" (p. 165). As he therapeutically adds, "Boredom is not a deprivation, the want of something to do; it is a positive act of repressing what is attractive but forbidden, and *then* there is nothing interesting to do" (p. 166).

Though Goodman insists on "practical" proposals to respond to our organizational disease, the larger part of his discussion is, reasonably enough, indictment. But he cites twice (pp. 24, 160) the key modern anarchist demand for Workers' Control—he calls it "collective contract" and direct management—though he doesn't develop it. He makes passing comments on "faculty control" of schools and universities (pp. 24, 161), and on giving students greater autonomy, including the freedom *not* to go to college when they lack intellectual motivation. Dispersal of the media and cultural institutions, he thinks, would counteract their extrinsic falsification by authority, exaggerated scale, absurd costs, and lack of true community functions (pp. 94 ff.). Some things, however, should not be decentralized, such as air traffic control and certain heavy industries (p. 9). Others—the automotive system, urban policy, provide examples—will probably have first to be further centralized so that they can be decentralized. Everywhere, of course, we could move toward more participation, delegated authority, self and group scheduling—and the recognition that "voluntary association has yielded most of the values of civilization" (p. 4).

Goodman strikingly answers the objection that decentralizing "puts too much faith in human nature" by reversing it: "We must avoid concentration of power because we *are* fallible" (p. 19) and because decentralized orderings may encourage "the potentialities of intelligence, grace and freedom in men." To such ends, we should force authority to decentralize, though he doesn't much say how, and encourage "spontaneous association" (p. 21). (His examples of the latter, from the 1960s Movement, now have some poignance.) To the loaded political question of how our society lessening its power-role will help the rest of the world, he sharply responds that "the export of our own high standard" of living and organization "is a form of neo-imperialism" (p. 170), and ultimately "the lesson of decentralizing is the formation of the world community on a basis of functional regions rather than national states" (p. 171). No doubt, but his actual concern has been far more limited and modest. "Since I am a conservative by disposition, I am not quite so ready to remake human nature (even according to my own blueprint), nor to scuttle the culture of the Western world" (p. 155), as are many radicals. Probably the liberal audiences admired this touchingly cautious-appearing anarchism, if not the iconoclastic views of most of their America.

The arguments for decentralizing remained central to all of Goodman's social criticism, though perhaps more narrowly in later years. As he restates it in his last book of social criticism: "The only prudent course is to try piecemeal to defend and extend the areas of liberty, locally, on the job, in the mores" (p. 197). From depowering and decentralizing, he expects that "local liberty will produce functional liberty" (p. 187)—a perhaps too optimistic fusion of freedom and efficiency. As with E. F. Schumacher, the small tends to have a special and absolute value in itself, but he fails to consider that the small-scale can also frequently be repressive and oppressive. Also earnest but not sufficiently serious is Goodman's citing the "Scandinavian or mixed economy" (p. 149)[25] as a model since he does not examine—to use his own key phrase discussed earlier—"the change of scale" to an American society more than several dozen times as large as such homogeneous and peripheral countries. And the tone comes out too blandly ameliorist at times to be anything but superficial: "Since all actual societies are, and have to be, mixtures of socialism, market economy, etc., the problem is to get a more judicious mixture and this *might* be more attainable by tinkering than by radical change" (p. 205). The patient with a massive invasive malignancy should tinker with his diet?

When not posing as prudent sage, Goodman responded more radically. As he sensed, "to eliminate the intermediary" (p. 199) in the grossly baroque American economy would be to eliminate a large part of it.[26] A major reduction in "the centralizing style" would be revolutionary. Given the conditions of our technocracy, "perhaps *no* central authority can be legitimate; it is bound to render the citizens powerless and to be dehumanizing" (p. 163). Yet the needed depowering (as he pointed out about transportation, the media, the cities), is so great as to require the legitimacy of massive change. Goodman wobbles, then—perhaps necessarily, for it is a true dilemma—between prudent local decentralizing and drastic social revolution. No wonder that in polemical addresses such as *Like a Conquered Province* Goodman sees "an empty and immoral empire" destroying the American "libertarian, pluralist, and populist" values (p. 25). The phony "pluralist" system of interlocking power groups merely accelerates the centralizing dominations.[27] Radical libertarian change is desperately needed and despairingly unlikely. Such, partly in spite of himself, was his serious message, and with that he really was a far-out anarchist.

IV *Patriot with a Black Flag*

"Anarchism is grounded in a rather definite social-psychological hypothesis: that forceful, graceful, and intelligent behavior occurs only where there is an uncoerced and direct response to the physical and social environment; that in most human affairs, more harm than good results from compulsion, top-down direction, bureaucratic planning, pre-ordained curricula, jails, conscription, states."[28] Put in this commonsensical way, one might feel that only the very fearful would strongly reject this libertarian-liberal emphasis, especially when, as Goodman usually held, this uncoerced condition should properly be arrived at "piecemeal." But truth to tell, a good many of us anarchist-minded doubt such substitution of social psychology for the ethics of liberty and equality and justice, and of liberal reform for social revolution.

However, as Paul Goodman explicitly identified himself in his last book of social criticism, *New Reformation* (1970), he was a "conservative anarchist" (p. 202). He not only affirms his allegiance to American Jeffersonian, populist, pragmatic, and progressive traditions, but to a more general positive American identification. He had exalted "patriotism" in *Growing Up Absurd* and many other works. But why would a partisan of anarchy reaffirm himself as a conservative American patriot?

Partly this emphasis came because he had gone "rather sour on the American young" radicals and their lack of patriotism. This includes repulsion to the authoritarian Leninism which seemed to be taking over the New Left, though several years earlier he had thought the Movement was "immune" to such totalitarianism.[29] Political and personal decline encourage him to the view that there is a general "breakdown of belief" and a consequent "cultural and religious crisis" (p. x). Rather self-flatteringly, he sees himself as the "Erasmanian skeptic" (p. xi) of the protest movement to which he has contributed and which has now become a "New Reformation." Not of the manipulative sort to be a hard new Luther or Cromwell, not radical enough to be a new Leveler or Digger or continuing antinomian spirit, he retreats to his identification as Man of Letters, though still a "citizenly" one in the tradition, he says, of John Milton (p. 202). Or: "As a man of letters, I am finally most like Coleridge (with a dash of Matthew Arnold when the vulgarity of liberalism gets me by the throat)" (p. 193). (While this may be pretentious, he also means that he was addicted to boys the way Coleridge was addicted to opium.) The models are certainly highfalutin conservative, especially for the turbulent late 1960s. With usual earnestness, Goodman did spend his remaining couple of years with the emphasis on Man of Letters, doing verse and literary ruminations. Such drawing back from the increasingly desperate radical styles of politics and freakishness of the counterculture was to become endemic with American intellectuals in the early 1970s.[30]

In partial contrast with the libertarianism of his earlier social criticism (such as the "integrated" paradigm of *Communitas*), Goodman now emphasized a confined-liberal view: "the aim of politics is to produce not a good society but a tolerable one" (p. 204). (In Chapter Three, I discuss his own earlier criticism of such meliorism.) In this disenchantment, anarchism serves more as distant informing spirit than as his politics. Yet it is in this period (1968–1972) that he becomes the establishment-recognized anarchist—not unlike the Kropotkin he admired (who had abandoned fundamental anarchism in patriotically affirming the Allies in World War I). Goodman now presented his version of libertarianism for the *New York Times Magazine*, the *Encyclopaedia Britannica, Religious Perspectives*, and similar conventional media. In one of these, "The Black Flag of Anarchism," he repeats his view that the international "student protest" of the late 1960s was essentially libertarian"—"the spontaneity, the concreteness of the issues, and the tactics of direct action are themselves characteristic of anarchism" (p. 203). He rightly notes that anarchist styles and values have "always been anathema to Marxist Communists" and "ruthlessly suppressed" (p. 204). But rather more dubiously, he denies that anarchism is "necessarily socialist, in the sense of espousing common ownership." While there have been "individualist," and even some contradictory "right-libertarians" who espouse "anarchocapitalism," most of anarchism for more than a century has been various modes of left-socialism—communist, mutualist, syndicalist.[31] Goodman is not intellectually clear on anarchist history here.

Neither, of course, are the ignorant "American young" who do not even know "the correct name for what they in fact do" (p. 205), which is not a question of ideological purity but of their confusion of Leninist "cadre" manipulation with libertarian rebellion. Goodman's main examples here are the authoritarian revolutionism of Students for a Democratic Society in the two Columbia protest-occupations of 1968. The Movement goals of "participatory democracy" were largely anarchist, as *were* the early methods of militancy (p. 209). The "delusional" coercive tactics of the Marxist sectarians did not entirely destroy this. He sensibly adds that "the arrogance, cold violence and inhumanity of our established institutions" are worse than the militants (p. 212).

In ambivalent responses to other aspects of the Movement, Goodman gives some slight praise to the counterculture, especially Emmett Grogan's Diggers, the Dutch Provos, and the antipolitical rebellions and subversions, but qualifyingly insists that their social vision is often "silly" or dangerous in accepting the technocratic ordering, for in the end "power will be wielded by the technocrats, and they themselves will be colonized like

Indians on a reservation."[32] He concludes with the conventional wisdom that a coherent freedom requires "worthwhile work, pursuing the arts and sciences, practicing the professions, bringing up children, engaging in politics" (p. 214). This, he admits, may be "old-fashioned, Calvinistic." But his condescendingly cursory treatment of much of the actual libertarianism of the time is more than generational. Put to the test, the late Goodman responds with deep conservativism, holding desperately to residual values of family and work and culture, however eccentric his allegiance to them, in a tone which denies millenarian belief in their replacement or re–creation.

In "Anarchism and Revolution"[33] Goodman takes a very broad view of the tradition: "Western history has had some pretty good anarchist successes; anarchy is not merely utopian dreams and a few bloody failures. Winning civil liberties, from Runnymede to the Jeffersonian Bill of Rights; the escape of the townsmen from feudal lords, establishing guild democracy; the liberation of conscience and congregations since the Reformation; the abolition of serfdom, chattel slavery, and some bonds of wage slavery; the freeing of trade and enterprise from mercantilism; the freedom of nations from dynasties and of some nations from imperialists; the development of progressive education and the freeing of sexuality–these bread-and-butter topics of European history are never called 'anarchist' but they are" (p. 216). As broad as his libertarian-liberalism is, an anarchist might note that it never includes deicide, feminism, and a good many other struggles against inequality and submission. Even within anarchisms, Goodman's preferences show an elitist cast; he usually emphasizes Kropotkinism (the legions of the skilled, the "professions") over Baukuninism (the legions of the outcast, the *lumpen*) as the force of liberation, though admitting that student anarchism usually tends to be Baukunist. His was middle-class libertarianism. What more radical tone surfaces usually relates to his "New Reformation" analogy–the breakdown of "legitimacy" and the "cultural crisis." That provides the revolution in the offing, and so he ends on the apocalyptic note that "we may be headed for a Thirty Years' War" (p. 232). But that was written in the late-1960s, with a not uncommon flourish as the American Vietnamese War, and the dissidence in the streets and institutions, continued. From a decade later, it looks poignantly melo-dramatic, and our crisis less protestant.

What Goodman meant by "New Reformation" was "an up-heaval of belief that is of religious depth, but that does *not* involve destroying the common faith, but to purge and reform it," for "we are not going to give up the mass faith in scientific technology that is the religion of modern times" (p. xi).[34] Besides the need for new professional and educational ethics, the crisis requires some new legitimatization of social ordering. While he repeats some of his arguments for decentralizing (pp. 182 ff.), he seems disenchanted with visionary thinking—"Unless it is high poetry, utopian thinking is boring" (p. 205)—thus eliminating much of his own earlier writing. Social criticism must still aim at "a practical effect"—the pretense to " 'neutral' sociology is morally repugnant and bad science"—but Goodman is finding it less to his purposes and feels more fearful: "Any violent collec-tive change would be certainly totalitarian, whatever the ideology" (p. 197). The implication seems to go beyond "violence" to any *drastic* change.

In a long, ragged essay of four chapters, "Legitimacy," which includes an irrelevant and uninsightful chapter-memoir on his war-resistor son killed in an accident in 1967, the issues seem beyond Goodman and muddled. There are some libertarian touches—as in the later note: "The excluded or repressed are always right in their rebellion, for they stand for our whole-ness" (p. 194). The obvious arguments against "foolish drug laws and other moral legislation" (p. 129), and the Kantian disclaimers against laws (such as military and racist) which deny moral agency are, unfortunately and dubiously, linked to claims that professional ethics (physicians', teachers', and so on) are exempt from the law (p. 131). Goodman seems to yearn, at times, for reestablishing "authority" in the "tonic American conception that the sanction of law is the social compact of the sovereign people" (p. 130). But his selective use of Jeffersonian and pragmatic traditions sees them as taking ambiguous views of law so to make "permanent nonviolent revolution possible" (p. 133). Thus racist and militaristic laws should be seen as "illegitimate" violations of the social compact (p. 138). Civil disobedience to them asserts the "General Will" (p. 137). Still, the issue may be moot since now "the Americans have accepted the void of sovereignty" (p. 140). Perhaps the uncertainty here covers his recurrent earlier argument that one should defy laws but *not* get punished for it, rather "go underground" since crisis conditions do not require principled behavior, established or revolutionary: "the politics and morality of apocalypse fall in between and are ambiguous" (p. 115). In *New Reformation* he adds that "civil disobedients are nostalgic patriots without available political means" (p. 141). Though himself a mild civil disobedient in encouraging draft resistance (unlike Spock et al., never prosecuted), what may be at issue here is his own patriotic malaise for the loss of American "legitimacy"![35]

He claims that what is ironically legitimate in an historical sense is "anarcho-pacifism"—"the philosophy of institutions without the State and centrally organized violence" (p. 143)—since only this has consistently opposed statism of all varieties which has "impeded rather than helped the advancing functions of civilization" (p. 144). True legitimacy must be based in "self-regulation and natural order" (p. 156)—again!—and "springs from liberty, some kind of free identification, and must start from local and occupational liberty" (pp. 179–80). Goodman's political anarchism, I take it from his loose mix of assertions, is merely expedient expression under plight of social anarchism. Paul Goodman had no larger politics than to try to maintain the "tolerable" by resistance, withdrawal, and protest while trying to further local and personal freedom.

But Goodman's antipolitics—a widespread view that political theorists give insufficient attention—seems trapped in the inability to find, anymore, the local and personal as separable from the worldwide "plight of modern times." In a late essay, "Confusion and Disorder" (1971; *Line*, pp. 233–45), he notes that as a society we are quite unable "to assimilate the quantum jumps of science, technology, urbanization, and complex organization" that dominate us. To that he admits, old and sick, "I don't know the answer" and then suggests a number of tangential ones on the general principles that "nature heals" and that we need "withdrawal and simplification" (p. 239). Consciously or not, this is taking the position of the traditional therapist-sage, such as Lao-tzu or Thoreau. Moral admonitions include limiting technology by the strictest "criteria of prudence, safety, modesty, common sense"—and so with social organization. Unschooling, decentralizing, and generally limiting massive change should be part of a willingness to "learn to tolerate disorder" in the coming society. In 1971 he expected, as did many, more disruptiveness than in fact developed. We might even see it as "promising when things fall apart," for "maybe some things will fall into their natural parts and recombine into more natural wholes." " 'Chaos is order' is an old anarchist epigram" (p. 245). In an earlier essay he had warned of "avoiding chaos which tends to produce dictatorship."[36] Perhaps he should have said that imposed order becomes chaos.

Anyway, playing upon the double meaning in "anarchism" may not be irrelevant. Neither may be the skepticism indigenous to it. An example, in his last public speech, is that anarchists are not optimists and do not believe "that human nature is good. . . . It's improvable, but probably lousy. People are corrupt as hell, therefore don't give anybody any power. . . . In fact we know by experience the more power people have the more corrupt they become. Let's make sure that everybody has an independent free-hold of their own, and if they've got that then there will be a limit to how bad things can get. . . . You don't want politics to give you a good society. All you want is a tolerable background so the important parts of life can go on" (pp. 271–72).[37]

This retreat from his earlier utopianism may be salutary in its skeptical modesty, though those who find themselves in political and social situations in which "the important parts of life" have difficulty in going on—without correcting the misorder to allow such meliorism—may not find this withdrawal, and emphasis on autonomy, a sufficient ethic for equality and community. The resistance to power has become passive. Such antipolitics, I believe, is rightly libertarian. But it demands antinomian direction, which means its allegiances belong only to the dissident and rebellious, local or universal, never to institutions and countries. Goodman's wobbly anarchism might be summarized by some little verses entitled "Black Flag" about a draft-resister rally under the anarchist emblem in which he looks toward the time when "the black flag is my country's spirit." The confused metaphor allows patriotism to undercut libertarianism.[38] The

black flag may not be his to take home—as the poem concludes—
but, like Diogenes's lamp, should always be carried mockingly
high. Still, Paul Goodman did carry the black flag into a number
of places and waved it before many people.

CHAPTER 3

The Therapeutic Gadfly

I Pursuits of Youth

PAUL Goodman's libertarianism, as he saw it, often took the
forms of a "therapeutic art."[1] Metaphors of therapy provided
a positive personal and public coloration to what might reasonably be viewed as a darkly drastic inconoclasm. A frequent
project of his therapeutic concern was American youth—schooling and education, psychology and protest politics, sexual and
social roles. In his most public years, the 1960s, Goodman was
the noted middle-aged doctor-prophet of that odd creation,
American adolescence, and its ambiguous crisis state from
thirteen to thirty. Behind his concern, as many of Goodman's
incidental comments and his verses insist, was a sense of deprivation and injury in his own youth. His pursuit of youth-issues
served as self-therapy as well as radical social therapeutics.
His compulsive homosexual pursuit of young males added an
obsessional tone to his concern.

The book of social criticism which made Paul Goodman
famous, and gave him the longed-for public role, was *Growing
Up Absurd*, subtitled "Problems of Youth in the Organized
System" (1960), which became a best-seller (in its first years
it sold more than 100,000 copies and remains in print nearly
two decades later).[2] This libertarian-tinged view of topical
social problems is not a good book, even within its limited
genre of pop-sociology, and is far from Goodman's best work.
Still, this rough and rambling essay around adolescent "delinquency"—really, American society's delinquency—offers some
suggestive insights and bits of a vision of a more authentic
society, something that can't be said for most sociological
writing.[3]

Growing Up Absurd derives from the popular mode of

65

sociological critiques of the 1950s, most specifically William
H. Whyte's *The Organization Man* (1956), which it inverts by
focusing on the fall-out victims of the processing structure,
urban delinquents and some other youth, rather than the suburban corporate personnel. (It was also partly styled by the pop-
radical gestures of *Commentary* at that time—since inverted
into pop-conservativism—in which it was partly serialized.)
It is a condescending mode—the superior expert analyzing
the strange folkways of his neighbors—which Goodman does
not altogether escape, including its obfuscating jargon, its
facile overgeneralizations, and its caricature typologies. But
Goodman does not slide into sociological scientism's claims
to "value-free" views. On this he scores some apt points: unlike their great predecessors in the previous century, "most of
our contemporary social scientists are not interested in fundamental social change" because, academics, they "do not like
to think that fighting and dissenting are proper social functions . . ." (p. 10). The social scientizers have also reified their
abstractions into a self-confirming reality. Thus the methodological pattern of "socialization" (as in Parsonian social theory)
replaces tangible truths of what it means to grow up by
circular needs of the system. Otherwise put, "Socialization to
what?" Is it to an inhuman system, or to a full human nature and
communal possibility? (pp. 8–11). "*Growth, like any ongoing
function, requires adequate objects in the environment,*" yet
"our abundant society is at present simply deficent in many of
the most elementary objective opportunities and worth-while
goals that could make growing up possible" (p. 12). Goodman, of course, assumes again a "nature of things," human and
social.

Though supposedly concerned with the young, Goodman
only allows for the male half of them. The crass justification for
this: "A girl does not *have* to, she is not expected to, 'make
something' of herself. Her career does not have to be self-
justifying, for she will have children . . ." (p. 13). By ignoring
girls, we are of course helping them, for "if the boys do not
grow to be men, where shall the women find men?" And what
other possible purpose in life could woman have? And even
among that male half, we may, apparently, ignore the well-to-do,

the nonurban, and a good many other males who do not appeal to Goodman's quaintly lusting sense of "lads" pursuing the "manly." That leaves three crude groupings: those submissively caught in the system's "rat race"; those demirebels against the system, "The Beats"; and those obvious victims of the system, urban "delinquents." Troubled boys.

A maturing male human nature, for Goodman, requires an accessible significant social identity mandated by vocation and community. "It's hard to grow up when there isn't enough man's work" (p. 17), by which he means the socially productive and morally confirming. Curiously, in his discussions of work Goodman assumes affluence and nearly full employment, ignoring our overpopulation and technological displacement and dehumanizing. His structural causes are moral and aesthetic, not economic, technocratic, and demographic, so that they must miss some of the issue.[4] Ours, he says with a criticism probably indebted to Thorstein Veblen, is "a system in which little direct attention is paid to the object, the function, the program, the task, the need; but immense attention to the role, procedure, prestige and profit." Consequently, work "is rarely done with love, style, and excitement, for such beauties only emerge from absorbtion in real objects" (p. xiii). Work becomes meaningless. "American society has tried so hard so ably to defend the practice and theory of production for profit and not primarily for use that now it has succeeded in making its jobs and profits profitable and useless" (p. 19). Neither Marxist nor capitalist ideologues concern themselves with the need for "the man-worthy job itself" (pp. 28, 37). Goodman wants to return to a Lutheran sense of "vocation," a Calvinistic sense of laboring as virtuous (pp. 139, 150). I think he quite fails to reckon not only with the variety of work attitudes in America but with the ravages of the Protestant Ethic (in spite of having read Max Weber). With uncomprehending righteousness, he looks back to Carlyle rather than forward to new notions of work and vocation.

While I agree that much in American society undercuts senses of worthwhile work and authentic vocation by a fraudulent emphasis on "role-playing," by commercial exploitation, and by rationalization and perpetuation of a technocratic system for its own sake, and that as a result many of the young (middle

class as well as "disadvantaged," young women as well as young
men) lack adequate access to genuine activity and to place in
a concerned community, Goodman's counterings and terms are
often dubious. For example, he asserts that the young need
models of "honor" such as represented by "great men" while
we just provide them "glamorous images with empty roles"
(p. 154). But isn't that what "great men" generally have been?
He should also have reread his own discussion of that great
libertarian philosopher Falstaff on "honor." Goodman's discussion
also tends to be moralistically thin in not, for example, recognizing the roles for honor and patriotism for the American
young of pro and semipro sports. A chapter devoted to "Patriotism" includes bathetic comments on George Washington, dishonest claims that American patriotism was not chauvinistic
until the twentieth century (ignoring the Mexican War, Indian
Wars, Civil War, and much else), and the fatuous glorification
of "space exploration"—"the adventure in space" now "makes
life worth the trouble again" (p. 104). Instead of arguing
against the degradations of national and historical patriotism,
which have had the fortunate side-effects of reducing some
vicious American parochialism, he should have, like a good
anarchist, argued for patriotic localism and a defiant universalism.

Besides greatness and patriotism, of course, we need
"DEMOCRACY" and the other obvious verities, so Goodman
capitalizes two dozen catch words (LIBERALISM, BROTHER-
HOOD, HONESTY, etc.) and with clichéd condescension writes
moralistic little paragraphs on them (pp. 218–25). In spite of
some devastating social criticisms, Goodman also falls back on
clichéd reformism; our problems are "precisely from the betrayal
and neglect of the old radical-liberal program" (p. 16), our
"compromised revolutions" (p. 217). A sharper critic would
have noted their irrelevancies, omissions and falsities instead
of blandly calling for a resoration of the "social balance" (p. xiv).
No wonder *Absurd* was popular, often substituting earnest moralisms for political seriousness.

Add the topical indignations (against rigged quiz shows), the
clichéd righteousness (against "the rat-race"), the condescending
sympathy (for the young and confused), and the virtuous edification (for the obvious and traditional), and much of the work

is better read as symptomatic than substantial. No one recalling the mainline temper of the late 1950s would argue with his sense of a claustrophobic society—"An Apparently Closed Room" (p. 159 ff.). His chapter on what rebels were publicly visible, the Beats—"The Early Resigned" (pp. 170–90) —insists they were "childish and parochial" and incapable of "art," though he does paternalistically praise their longings for autonomous leisure, responsiveness, and community. He later even describes them as "crazy young allies" (p. 241) in the hope of improving American society—a reversal of tone as well as roles. Since he misuses the Beat lingo (man, cool, drag), has little sense of jazz and the rest of the subculture—he cutely suggests that they take up Balinese dancing (p. 188), a ritual art which couldn't be less appropriate—his case on Beat lack of culture and intelligence could hardly be persuasive even if right.[5] His own style of bohemians (included under the rubric of "Independents") were not all that much better. But Goodman is better when less threatened, by competing bohemians, in discussing another type of young, the urban delinquents— "The Early Fatalistic" (pp. 191–215)—who have little option in their lack of jobs, culture, or other possibilities, but compulsively to defy, and to get caught and punished. They do pay the price of "the system."

Now and again Goodman's stumbling accounts are lifted up by insights. For example, he makes the nice discrimination about adolescent behavior that *"doing the forbidden is a normal function of growth"* (p. 131) but that "raising the ante" in dangerousness is "a sign that a person is not in contact with his real needs" and is therefore turning self-destructive. This, he notes, not only applies to juveniles but to essentially adolescent, even if older, types such as "middle-mangement" people and President John F. Kennedy and the like.

Goodman, of course, favors sex for the young, but also perceives the falsification of the sexual revolution in that 1950s "permissiveness combined with withdrawal from real contact precisely produces the sexual-sadistic need" (p. 125) so dominant in popular culture which commercially exploits and further warps it. At times here, Goodman is still the sexual-social libertarian. He scores the ideology of the 1950s, the middle-class family "togetherness"—"one can't pass on a middle-class standard with-

out believing in its productive and cultural mission" (p. 123),
and most people don't, really.[6] Indeed, American suburbanism
uses family affirmation as a substitute for other values, a privateering ersatz-morality. Many marriages should dissolve for
the well-being of all involved; "the partners would suddenly
become brighter, rosier and younger" (p. 120).[7] But we have so
denuded social forms that we have little in the way of other
modes "for secure sex, companionship, and bringing up children."

Growing Up Absurd, then was a sometimes insightful but often
ill-organized, clichéd, and superficial piece of topical social
criticism. It did not seriously analyze the problems of vocation
and community for the young in an overpopulated technocracy.
Goodman's better remarks—they are not developed arguments—
on schooling religiosity (discussed below) and decentralizing
(discussed before), were better developed in other writings.
However, *Absurd's* public influence in focusing attention on dis-
contents of the young and the lack of humane values in much
of our technocracy, from a sometimes radical perspective, may
well have been salutary.[8]

No doubt the public gadfly performances that followed from
Goodman's fame as the author of that book had some merit.
Such would be to emphasize in a lecture, "Vocational Guidance,"[9]
that educators ought to be in conflict with the economic system
in guiding the young towards vocations: "The criterion of socially
useful work attacks our profit system. The criterion of a job that
exercises capacities and offers a field for real training and sub-
sequent initiative is pretty close to Syndicalism, it threatens management" (p. 262). But one hardly expects counseling and placement people to feel more than a twinge of conscience at this
radical edification within a conventional context. Perhaps the argument of a somewhat better piece, "Youth Work Camps," had
more possible practicality in suggesting that America should
create communities of adolescents, in place of family and schooling controls, "akin to the Youth House of primitive cultures
(p. 264), plus useful and honorable work in "the public real
world" (p. 266), including "urban conservation and urban re-
newal" as well as rural work and remaking all the ugly small
towns of America (p. 272).

Dr. Goodman's pursuit of youth issues also led to an earnest paternalism about rising student rebelliousness in the early 1960s. In "Crisis and New Spirit" he saw student dissatisfaction—and pandemic plagiarism—as response to a cheating and manipulative society with a "foolish economy and a monstrous war machine" (p. 277). No doubt he was right that some of the young were re-actively discovering that "community is possible, we need not be fragmented individuals in a system out of human scale" (p. 286). He hopes the young will develop a "practical" and nonideological idealism. Such seemed to be the Berkeley Free Speech Movement of 1964, and its aftermath. In a long report a few months later, "Berkeley in February,"[10] he viewed the rebellion partly in terms of his theme in *Absurd* that "the dominant system" in the university as in the society "is not moral enough to grow up into" (p. 127). The Movement seemed to him confirmation that *"free-dom and meaning will outweigh anomie"* in a spreading revolt (p. 128). The prediction, of course, was correct. On the whole, he was positive about the student demands for more honesty, freedom, relevance, solidarity, and reforms. He took them as confirming his pursuit of youth as the bearers of values: *"the thoughts and feelings of the young have been more relevant to the underlying realities of modern times"* (p. 140) than that of other groupings in the society. While Goodman's reportage seems to me less incisive than that of Wolin, Rossman, and others at the time—he does draw upon them—and his tone is sometimes condescending—"They know what freedom is—yes, they do—but they don't really know what a university is" (p. 144)—he saw the Movement as affirming the possibility of academic, and broader social, change. Goodman was to sympathize with the campus rebellions for a few more years; the attraction was mutual and he lectured at hundreds of universities, especially as a radical school reformer.

II *Unschooling the Young*

With *Growing Up Absurd* and his related gadfly-to-youth ac-tivity, Goodman had found a public and literary role which answered his craving for attention from young men as well as the intellectual establishment. He had, in his fifties, found a fashion-able vocation and proceeded to write many lectures and essays,

and several ragged books, around American schooling. It was
not a new subject for him since resistance to conventional schooling had been highlighted in several of his early novels, *The Grand
Piano* and *Parents' Day*, and his version of the "progressive"
tradition in education had been central to his social psychology
and anarchism as well as his personal concern.

Perhaps an appropriate fancy of Paul Goodman as educator
might be of an unwashed Jewish monk presiding over a seminar
in a slum park with Aristotle's *Logic* in one hand and Reich's
Sexual Revolution in the other. With a mixture of Latin tags
from Aquinas, misused hip slang, quotations in the originals from
Rilke and Genet, Yiddishisms, and jargon from American sociology and psychoanalysis, he propounds Kafka's art as psychotic
prayer and the social therapy of tribal communes for adolescent
boys in depopulated rural America. It would be part of a communal antiuniversity, simultaneously vanguardist and antique,
ritualistic and unbuttoned, marked by curiously moral professional learning and eager homosexual groping—earnestly outrageous.

For when Paul Goodman wrote in his last year, "I don't believe
in modern universities," it may have been a notation of despair
for one who saw himself as above most things "a university man"
who yearned for an ancient "community of scholars."[11] At that
time he was a visiting professor at the University of Hawaii, an
enlarging academic factory, though he had predicted the year
before, apparently with pleasure, that soon some "of the ex-
panded neo-Classic community colleges and State universities
will become ghost towns."[12] As a poor Jewish boy, strongly identifying with schooling, who was a bright major in philosophy
at the City College of New York in its heyday and who spent
years as a graduate student in literature and philosophy at the
University of Chicago in the Hutchins era, where he eventually
completed his doctorate, and who taught and lectured at hundreds of American universities (though he never managed to
hold a regular academic appointment), one might think he had
a personal and even an intellectual vested interest in American
higher education. He did, and that is why he wanted to shut
much of it down.

Some of Goodman's elitist-libertarian notions of the true university—paradigmatic for much of his sense of community—may have come from the love-hate yearning of the hotly graceless outsider who had yet, he thought, proved that he really belonged to a superior communion of the learned. But his criticisms of much of prevalent American hired learning also reveal a broader seriousness, and anti-schooling polemics probably provided his most influential role.[13] It is a sometimes puzzling critique because of its two antithetical foundations. In one direction, Goodman displays the pious methodological pedant, quoting and twisting the earliest recorded Greek one, practicing his version of Chicago-style neo-Aristotelianism in literary study, and repeatedly proposing to return the university to some facsimile of its medieval form by taking most earnestly its trappings of ancient clerical duty, international self-governing community, and disputatious religious brotherhood of male (only) masters-scholars.

In the other direction, which has usually been in scornful opposition to such "scholasticism," was his Progressive Education.[14] This he saw as the continuing tradition of Rousseau, Jefferson, Kropotkin, Veblen, Dewey, Neill, and the recent radically "permissive" American schooling experiments (on which, indeed, he had some influence). For Goodman, progressivism had failed in not going far enough in the direction of learning-by-doing and pervasive educational democracy; moral cowardice and the "administrative mentality" had corrupted it, as had the anti-intellectual "adjustment ethic" and the ideological subordination to the suburban-corporate-technological. However, conflict between the old-academic and the progressive traditions surfaces now and again, as when he criticized A. S. Neill for a "latitudinarian lack of standards" in intellectual matters, or when he scorned his student sympathizers for preferring Rock to Bach and *Howl* to *Paradise Lost*.[15] Perhaps his traditionalism with the radicals, like his radicalism with the traditionalists, went beyond hostile role-playing to something shaped like conservative revolution. Past libertarians often took views which in effect *extended* formal education, even from Godwin's rationalistic theories of learning through Tolstoy's founding of peasant schools and Ferrar's program for the Modern School to many recent attempts in America at "freeing" schools but not people from them. The once radical desire to give access to the underclasses to educational power

against monarch and church went with an enlightenment faith
in literacy and the supposedly rational culture that would follow
from it. But universal free education, a demand in most past
anarchist manifestos, is no longer appropriate for universal
liberation when "schoolism" provides the ideology of control.
Thus now, anarchism versus schoolism.

Goodman's libertarian antiacademic rhetoric often aimed at
other "school-monks." By this he meant not so much traditional
faculty, whom he tended to treat a bit gingerly, than their replacement by "administrators and scholars with administrative
mentalities."[16] The bureaucratic and the time-serving—the anti-
intellectual academic majority—maximize corruptions: statist research and corporate servicing; the "imposed order" which
defines schooling within the competitive and controlling American social norms; and the aggrandizement of "the academic
machine for its own sake."[17] The university has primarily become
a bureaucratic factory for producing bureaucrats. It serves and
perpetuates the whole "New Class" of schooled technicians and
certificated professionals and indoctrinated managers—now "society is run by mandarins"—with their manipulative ideology for
more and more compulsory education and arbitrary expertise.
Academic careerists doing "methodical busy work" drive out the
impassioned intellectual and the original, and often *outré*, scholar.
Universities become major enemies of intellectual excellence.[18]
Furthermore, over-rewarded hierarchies of controlling school-
monks certified by academia threaten to academicize all of life,
from sex hygiene to international production, from media entertainment to universal war. "The old monkish invention of formal
schooling is now used as universal social engineering."[19]

This processing must be opposed, from the psychologically in-
jurious grading system through the academic job certification,
and from the state-submissive curricula and research to the in-
tellect-swamping mass custodialism. A large majority of the
students in the universities and colleges "ought not to be academically educated." Only a fool would deny it. Most of these
students "want and need another structure and identity, that
only an objective task and some other kind of community can
give them."[20] And even the remainder should be in the universities later: "College training, generally, should follow—not pre-

cede—entry [at an apprentice level] into the professions." "University education—liberal arts and the principles of the professions —should be reserved only for adults who already know something about which to philosophize."[21] (Which does not mean custodialism for the old—now often urged by self-interested educationists as if there were no shape in life outside of schooling!)

In a perhaps exaggerated but revealing statement for a longtime student of philosophy and literature, he rejects them: "I have not heard of any method whatever, scholastic or otherwise, of teaching the humanities without killing them."[22] Perhaps more pertinently, he notes that the "culture which we have inherited is by now in total confusion," which hardly leaves it teachable. Teaching high culture requires that it be "re-created in spirit or it is a dead weight on present spirit, and then it does produce timidity, pedantry, and hypocrisy," and so is "better forgotten."[23] Most science, also, is not best learned in the corrupt "porkbarreling" universities but on the job (technology), in the field (ecology), or in autonomous efforts ("shoestrong science") which encourage independence and initiative.[24] As for much of the remaining faculty, they won't do, either, since "college teaching is not itself a profession"—in the sense of medicine or architecture—and we need the clear standard that "the college teacher is a professional who teaches," a returned "veteran" of the more elaborate crafts, a philosophical practitioner back in the academic "walled city" to reflect upon and pass on his guild wisdom.[25] Though iconoclastic about the academic humanities and sciences, Goodman is unthinkingly, and contradictorily, pious about the other learned professions. Contrary to most evidence, he assumes the wisdom and disinterest of the specialist practitioner, and forgets that "professionalism" tends to be one of the most dehumanizing elaborations of the division of labor.

If consistent, Goodman would have generally eliminated universities. But after all, for some time they have been eliminating themselves by turning the higher schooling into a monstrous "bureaucratic trap" of antiintellectual custodialism, monkish racketeering, and social certification and indoctrination. No wonder the student rebellions of the 1960s were essentially "prison riots."[26] The system goes on less because of true educational function than because, like much else in the American economy,

it engages in self-rationalization and self-perpetuation—the ultimate Weberian bureaucracy. In this "official superstition" and
"wrong religion" of endless schooling, the inappropriate destroys
what good might be by "dilution and stupefying standardization."
This goes beyond waste since "the long schooling is not only
inept, it is psychologically, politically, and professionally, damaging."[27] It also destroys the few things the university can truly
do, such as provide "havens for those scholarly by disposition."[28]
As 1960s militants chanted for rather lesser reasons: "Shut it
down!"

Goodman's case against the universities, of course, is broadly
generalized. In the more muddled realities of an exploitative and
anomic society the *inefficient* academic bureaucracies do allow
some little place for true humanities and sciences and some small
sanctuary for the unwanted young and a remnant of authentic
intellectuals.[29] Still, I think his charges against academia were,
and remain, essentially true. He was probably right that even
the positive functions of the universities might often be better
carried out in a variety of other ways—sciences in the work
places and institutes, the humanities in the media and elsewhere,
the learning young and the critical intellectuals everywhere.
Goodman often sounded like an educational reformer—get rid
of the custodialism and alienating bureaucratization; free the
academic from the corrupting statist research and corporate
servicing—when he was really propounding broad social revolution.

Some of Goodman's tone seems conservative, as with his neo-
Aristotelianism, his intellectualism which anti-intellectuals mistake for social elitism, his rather quaint metaphors of the medieval
university, and his incongruously pious tastes in the humanities
and sciences. Because of the curious historical development of
American "liberalism," those who oppose more money for administrators and insist on limiting institutional functions, as
libertarians do, get misviewed as reactionaries. Reactive Goodman certainly was, though not in the bigoted sense of the usual
American political "right." He apparently sometimes thought he
was serving as a traditionalist reformer, recalling the universities
to ancient functions.[30] But the sweeping condemnations and
demands for changes insist that nothing less than the radica'

transformation of the whole ideological and institutional order will do. And this is far more radical than most Marxist-tinged views of indoctrinating education or liberal-colored views of social administering.

In one direction, Goodman demanded a dissenting academy—"the community of scholars must confront society, often in conflict." In another, he had some "practical proposals" for higher education, perhaps to assuage his sense of outlandishness by seeming "realistic," and to allay his anxious pessimism. In *Community of Scholars*, for example, he proposed "secession" with half-a-dozen professors, along with some community professionals, and 150 students going off to found an autonomous college. But they would not be so far from the established university that they couldn't use some of the facilities. Such libertarian-traditionalist colleges would be riding piggy-back on the established system but dispensing with *"external control, administration, bureaucratic machinery, and other excrescences that have swamped"* the academic.[31] Charming, but this makes many dubious assumptions (and not just in the rather literal-minded financial figures), such as that the established bureaucracies would tolerate it. He also foolishly assumes that faculty are not more conservative than the merely manipulative administrators, that most of the good but not especially popular faculty would not get wiped out, that a traditional education can be produced in a nontraditional community, and that where there is a discontented will there is an obvious communal way. Such notions of Goodman's presuppose the communal ideology which they must create and which would require a stronger faith and social purpose than the just vestigial humanistic-educational values. He obliquely responded later to such criticisms, and perhaps to the intervening experiences in the middle 1960s of the "Free Universities" which sometimes drew upon his very arguments but quickly descended into either political agitprop, which soon properly led the militants back into the streets, or into the mushy culture of "the freaks" —occultism, cute games and hobbies, psychopathic "self-expression," and cult therapies.[32] Goodman admitted in the late 1960s, in *New Reformation*, that such intentional communities as his secessionist colleges would rarely be possible in just educational terms. "A community finally has to have its own poetry" was his

curiously understated way of putting the need for a powerful
social and religious motivation.[33] Probably to create successfully
such small societies the larger society—the madly homogenizing
America with its schooling religiosity—would have to be signifi-
cantly changed. To be taken seriously, Goodman's "practical
proposals" in education must be seen as institutional-reformist
gestures of the social revolutionary. But, rightly enough, he left
no doubt that the universities should radically change and drastically shrink for better education and a better society.

III   More Unschooling of America

The radicalism of Goodman's educational reforms, his schooling
abolitionism, appears even more emphatic at the level below the
universities, perhaps because that called forth less subterranean
personal identification, and no classical and medieval models. At
his last public speech (1972), he said in answer to a question
about reforming secondary education, "we should abolish the
high schools, period."[34] He grants that "a few really academic
kids, 2 or 3% of the population," will no doubt still "go to little
academies." But "an academic environment is not the appropriate
means of education for most young people, including most of the
bright."[35] Indeed, as he correctly noted elsewhere, much of the
work of freshman college teachers is to try to get the students to
unlearn what little they have acquired in the schools. They resented learning it, resent unlearning it, and end with covert resentment as a major schooling experience. His countersuggestion,
in an earlier article: "The high schools are especially worthless;
the money should be put directly in the pockets of adolescents if
they are doing anything useful for themselves or society. . . ."[36]

Goodman, of course, does not consider such major secondary-
educational activities as sports, dating, doping, and the rest of
adolescent culturation, which could most likely be better done in
another environment than the schools. And so could real learning.
The high schools can't really be remedied. "I do not see any functional way to recruit a large corps of [good] high school teachers."[37] Few adults have the right responsive relation to adolescents
in the schooling sitituation, and fewer continue it; even the best
tend to sink into bureaucratically frustrated resignation. The cur-

riculum (that usual regenerative focus of the reformer) must become poorer and poorer "because an honest educator cannot seriously believe that the social sciences and the humanities are life-relevant to the average" of the mass of mis-motivated students in custodial care for bureaucratic mind-rinsing.[38] The outside pressures (parental and commercial and political exploitations) further reduce learning possibilities. In addition, "Commercially debauched popular culture makes learning disesteemed."[39] So does the understandably defensive "youth culture," which after all intends resistance "*against* the adults" by those alienated into a narrow and powerless sub-culture.[40] As Goodman repeatedly noted, with a pained sympathy for the young, the school processing lacks a sense of worldly reality just when that is most needed by the young. Instead of relating to that larger sense of things, "everything is preparation, nothing realization and satisfaction" (except in the synthetic ways of the substitute worlds of youth culture, sports, and the like). So the seeking self loses confidence, interest, responsiveness, and ends in "bafflement and nausea."[41] Thus frustrated, many students *develop* inabilities to learn, an acquired schooling "stupidity." In answer to this, the school-monks multiply remedial levels, or try fatuous gimmicks such as "teaching machines," or add more extrinsic motivations and punishments, including more schooling by compulsion.[42] The spread of bad schooling drives out the good. For all but a small minority of adolescents, our schooling becomes imprisoning, dulling, anti-intellectual, dis-spiriting, wasteful; it "arrests growth" (encouraging our characteristic permanent adolescence) and does other "positive damage to the young."[43] Simply abolishing secondary schooling would be a positive service.

But, as usual, Goodman tosses around some "practical proposals." Some of these, as with higher education, appear reformist, such as eliminating obvious coercions which do psychological damage as well as destroy intrinsic motivations. Thus the falsely competitive and anxiety-inducing exams and grading should go, as should—it necessarily follows—mandatory attendance, the overloaded scheduling, the behavior-controlling administering, the rigid ordering, and many of the imposed pieties toward institutions. Since Goodman wrote, a few changes have developed; some, such as "equivalency" exams for leaving school early, from the top (at least in California in the mid-1970s); others, from the bottom, include pandemic plagiarism (in the colleges, too), "grade inflation," heavy truancy, internal as well as external dropping out, and other modes of natural resistance to the excessive school processing. But, to my knowledge, most of the problems Goodman discussed remain basically the same.

Goodman did not really explore reforms. He had almost nothing to say about more interesting curricula for the high schools; the selection and preparation of teachers, school democratization to eliminate administrators, and other partial changes that could flow from his criticisms. For his real concern was with other ways of learning than by school processing. Though he appeared partly reformist (as in speaking to educationist groups) and partly conservative (as in testifying against more federal schooling money before a congressional committee), the real direction was toward social revolution.

Abolishing the high schools raises "other ways of entry for the young" into adult social realities. "Other kinds of youth communities should take over the social functions of the high school," for "our aim should be to multiply the paths of growing up" instead of concentrating on schooling.[44] Even if we let 10 percent or so (the usual estimate of the academically gifted) do work in languages, mathematics, and other traditional disciplines, there should be half a dozen other ways than schools for other youths. Among Goodman's "practical proposals" (often, as with much of his argument, only casually sketched): an extensive youth works corps (less military and more varied than the CCC of the 1930s); modern urban versions of the primitive "youth house," with autonomous support; kibbutz-style communes which integrate the young into the ongoing work of a dedicated community; nonschooling educational programs developed to service local culture (media, theater, and other arts); and vast apprenticeship programs not only in the trades and crafts but in all modes of technology and the professions.[45]

Goodman did not concern himself with the anti-apprentice ideologies, such as that for reasons of invidious hierarchy and control modern corporations and other bureaucracies prefer discrete prior class conditioning; the disjunctions of schooling/employment, like the suburb/work schizophrenia, heightens functional mobility and manipulateable anomie. Also, Goodman's early proposals for apprenticeships were patently by someone with no experience as an apprentice, and with little historical sense of why some apprenticing declined—it was tyrannical and exploitative in ways in which the bland school-processing could not so obviously be. Implicitly admitting the criticism, Goodman later granted that apprenticeships, private or governmental, were socially and morally ambiguous in our society because they put "the young under the control of the employer." Therefore, we "must design apprenticeships that are not exploitative," and that encourage critical participation—another version of anarchist "worker's control."[46] Once again, a practical educational reform turns toward libertarian revolution.

Surely some of Goodman's suggestions seemed reasonable within the current context. American politicians have advocated, and even partly developed, "youth corps" proposals, though usually protectively distant (in foreign countries, ghettos or wilderness), noncompetitive with the schools (for drop-outs, delinquents, or postgraduates), and sufficiently small in number and funding *not* to make a substantial difference in the society and its schooling pieties and controls. It may be that since Goodman wrote apprenticeships and other vocational emphases have increased (certainly academic humanities have drastically declined), though, sadly, still often dominated by the "school-monks." The young themselves have shown some initiative toward communal forms, resistance to endless schooling (or increased moratoria), and a spreading disenchantment with the "spirit-mashing" school processing, However, the conditions that Goodman deplored from the early 1960s to the early 1970s still seem largely present, which may tell us that American schooling remains ideologically and institutionally necessary for social control.

Goodman argued that "incidental education," that is, what one organically learns in games and rituals with one's peers and acquires from adults in community activities and socially significant work, constitutes the larger part of real education—not what is shoveled in classrooms.[47] Thus real educational reform would less come from improving the schools than from making "our whole environment more educative," including more open access for the young. Instead, in the 1960s at least, what Goodman viewed as the fatuously reactive youth-culture enlarged. This was how empty "adolescent society jealously protects itself against meaning," with its cultish lingo and rituals of the powerless insulating passivity and flight from commonsensical reality. The traditional humanist shows through here: without some deep connection with the fuller Western high culture, "one becomes trivial and finally servile."[48] Protective-exploitative youth culture "prevents ever being grown up." But what American schools consider growing up consists of institutional submission and petty-bourgeois character. Intellectually, much of schooling is disastrous, damaging "intrinsic motivation" and most full development. Learning "incidentally," on the other hand, will have the dangers of freedom: "choices along the way will be very often ill-conceived and wasteful, but they will express desire and immediately meet reality, and therefore they should converge on right vocation more quickly than any other course."[49] And not incidentally, result in more responsive people.

But what of the much-broadcast values of the schools as mechanisms for "socialization," from the Americanization of immigrants through the "raising-up" to middle-class access of the "minorities" and other poor? The immigrant issue, which led to some of the fervent expansion of schooling, is largely done with (except for such groups as the Hispanics, with whom it doesn't seem to be working very well). As for the contemporary poor, "It would probably help to improve the educational aspiration and educability of poor youngsters to give the money to poor families *directly*, rather than to channel it through school systems or other social agencies that drain off most of it for the . . . middle-class" servicing professionals. As Céline used to note dryly, "The poor need money." As Goodman also notes, with his frequent multiple suggestiveness, the poor should be given improved access to *all* institutions rather than just fobbed-off with the schools as a substitute for egalitarian justice. Or our society could properly "pension the poor," or it could make decent poverty reasonably possible and humane instead of the hasseling and self-degradation which subsistence living necessarily becomes in our warped affluence.[50]

For the earlier years of schooling, Goodman does not advocate abolition or sweeping reduction. The affluent society could more generously provide babysitting from six to twelve. At that age children need sanctuary from the family—Oedipal escape—in a permissively protective environment. He allows a schooling context for this, though with an emphasis on guided activities outside formal school scenes, in proper progressive tradition, which requires minimizing administration and furthering local control. Goodman had a whole bag of concretely sensible proposals, partly based on actual schools, for this loosening up of the system.[51] Learning requires varied experiments and possibilities with small classes under sympathetic young semiamateurs who like children (rather than the indoctrinees of Schools of Education) in a child-concerned curriculum. (The larger developmental pattern: child-focused in the early years, social activity-focused in the adolescent years, intellectual subject-focused in the mature years.) The lock-step structuring, and its examining and grading, must go, as must sexual and creative repression. Given a freely stimulating environment, children will naturally learn—learning to speak one's native language is the model here. Illiteracy must be the result of reactive stupidity, resistance, in our word-assaulting culture (*New Reformation*, pp. 98, 95). The lack of learning curiosity must be an engendered pathological condition. Even if the society wants to demand of its schools "uniform standards of achievement," it should recognize that "they cannot be reached by uniform techniques."[52] So even at this level, compulsory schooling and controls must also be rejected as antithetical to encouraging responsive children.[53]

Coercive social ordering provides the libertarian crux of Goodman's educational views. He combined his traditionalist humanism with progressive education, usually viewed as opposed, by advocating the elimination of coerced schooling of any kind. Liberating most students—and faculty—from the high schools and universities would leave progressive schooling in the early years not as hierarchical preparation (a source of the submission syndrome) but as partial liberation from the family into natural wider responsiveness. What formal higher education remained would be, by conventional American standards, for an intellectual elite, that is, for those dedicated to "humanities superior to power and success." The rest of learning for the young would be put back where it belongs, into the varied ongoing institutions of society—perhaps

even eliminating "youth" as a class and a subculture and a
pathology.

We may recognize again that Goodman's apparent reforms,
both conservative (academic) and progressive (primary), direct
us to radical social change—schooling abolitionism. Rightly sus-
picious of American reformist changes which rationalize and re-
enforce the coercive schooling mania, Goodman sometimes even
warned against improvements: the "practical social problem is . . .
not how to establish good schools but . . . how to keep it [society]
from enslaving whatever good education happens to be occur-
ring."[54] On the good anarchist premise that education is a
"natural" function, we must unschool America to allow it to
better learn.

IV   *Teasing the Technologues, and Other Animadversions*

Some of the most horrible failures of American education appear evident in our technological subserviences and manias. As
an Enlightment-styled Man of Letters, Paul Goodman took an
interest in, though hardly with profound knowledge, modern
science. He rather antiquely admired science as "natural philosophy" and the technological heroics of the days of the self-made
inventors such as Michael Faraday.[55] However, as a contemporary
American social critic his enthusiasm necessarily bore the heavy
burdens of scientific technology as central to militarism, over-
development, hierarchical giganticism, pervasive social control,
and dominating magical expertise. In the late-1960s Goodman
also acquired ecological concerns from other Movement critics.
Moralizing the spirit of early modern science yet oppressed by
some of the results, Goodman was caught in teasing ambivalences
and muddles.

In an essay at the beginning of the 1960s, " 'Applied Science'
and Superstition" (in *Utopian*), Goodman argued that the loss of
humanistic values (and science as part of the humanistic) put
technology out of humane control: "With us, the idea of a 'scientific society' seems to have degenerated to applying the latest
findings of professional experts to solve problems often created
by the ignorance of the mass, including science" (p. 24). He
wanted a technology decentralized and simplified for humane

choice. The public, indoctrinated by the state and commercial interests, takes a superstitious view, with scientists as "unconcerned priests" and many of "the machines used are, effectually, canned rituals" (p. 48). This sense of scientific technology as religiosity seems insightful; so does his positing libertarian requirements (from Geddes, Mumford, Borsodi, etc.) of relevance and amenity—or as Illich was later to say, "tools for conviviality." But Goodman's idolatry of Western science as moral virtue and knowledge undercuts the criticisms. Thus: "absolute freedom and encouragement—including a blank check—should be given to the pursuit of scientific knowledge, and yet the mass application of this knowledge ... should be highly selective and discriminating" (p. 26). He doesn't really consider how each tends to bleed into, or control, the other, and that there perhaps cannot be, in modern social organization, substantial separation of his "virtuous" science and the destructive technology that goes with it.

In a lecture a few years later, "The Morality of Scientific Technology"(in *Province*), Goodman attacks both the antitechnological views and the current statist-corporate control of technology. All he can counter with is decentralizing and urging rather puritanic ethics upon the technologues.[56] Several years later, in the lengthy discussion "Sciences and Professions" (in *New Reformation*), Goodman turns the technologues into heroes for resisting abuse of science and as the locus for a new *professional* ethics. He has to pretend, against the larger evidence of self-aggrandizing professional monopolies, that modern "professionals are autonomous men, beholden to the nature of things and the judgement of their peers" and dominated by duties to "benefit their clients and the community" (p. 47). (Is that why American professionals are greedily over-compensated and vehemently antagonistic to "nonprofessional" choices and independence?) Goodman also expresses patronizing outrage that other radicals don't seem impressed by the possibilities of reinstituting a medieval craft guild ethos which would make scientific technologists "responsible for the uses of the work they do" (p. 17).[57] But since apparently even most outstanding scientists show little of this ethical responsibility, the view is foolish as well as a drastic denial of control by community democracy.[58]

Goodman makes good negative points about scientific tech-

nology: the military abuse of science; the overtechnologization of
every advanced country to the detriment of the quality of life;
the failure to limit appropriately technology in developing areas—
Schumacher's "intermediate technology"; the built-in failures of
"Big Science" to be self-correcting, modest, autonomous; and the
egregious misuses of "behavioral sciences" for social control instead of individual and community service. He also dismisses a
weary argument, the "two cultures" of C. P. Snow, with "there
is only one culture" and "unless technology is itself more humanistic and philosophical, it too is of no use" (p. 12). Less justly, he
dismisses such arguments as Jacques Ellul's, that there may be
inherent dominations in modern technology, by simply insisting
that a decentralist philosophy answers it (p. 20).

But even this he lacks here. Instead, he has a sentimental bias
towards "shoestring science" (p. 15), which seems as irrelevant as
his call for transcendent professional ethics in the conditions of
technocracy. Goodman's rather stock and thin recapitulation of
earlier science confirms his inadequate sense of the issues.
Granted, he is bothered that perceptive thinkers in the existential
and libertarian traditions saw that scientific technology "would
become a new established superstition, incalculably dangerous"
(p. 41), but all he can do is call for a return to an earlier—and
probably nonexistent—moral puritanism of scientists. Ignorance
of the history and philosophy of science may account for some
of Goodman's difficulties such as his assumptions of monolithic
system and continuity of science instead of, for example, con-
flicting and changing "paradigms" (Thomas Kuhn, *The Structure
of Scientific Revolutions*). Thus he can only tease and muddle
the obvious.

Part of Goodman's inadequacy comes from what he calls the
technocratic "disease of modern times" (p. 22). He sees it as
pervasive, not just confined to America or capitalism. And he,
too, has it. In the 1950s he praised the "space program"; in *Absurd*
he exalted in the patriotic "adventure" of space exploration; and
he never did recognize (as Hannah Arendt and others long before
pointed out) the near psychotic nature of those desires to escape
our actual world. He treats contemptuously other radicals' objections—to space junketing and junk, to its political "circus" and
social irrelevance. Goodman fails to see the self-condemning irony

in his superstitious view of space vehicles—"these are our cathedrals." Certainly he is bothered by this dubious religiosity at times, half-recognizing that the space-mania depended on the very Big Science which he had elsewhere scorned and the centralized technological processing by state and corporations which violated his sense of ethical limits; yet he feels that "if this collective enterprise [the space-mania] is necessary for the on-going human adventure, we must go with it or commit historical suicide." How align technological decentralizing and its worst technocratic opposite? Obviously we can't, and so perhaps "we *are* at a dead end" (p. 32). Surely Goodman's superstitious thinking about science is.

Goodman seems better at a simpler level of technological effect, as with his well-known baiting of technocratic style, "Banning Cars from Manhattan" (1961; again with Percival Goodman).[59] This utopian-practical proposal outlines necessary and emergency access, and effectively eliminates the automobile from the central city in order to return street and parking land to community use, put people closer to work and services, restore neighborhoods, and enhance the health, comfort, and the amenity of urban life. This admirable proposal also intends to illustrate a social philosophy of planning: "*The aim of integral planning is to create human scale community, of manageable associations, intermediary between the individuals and families and the metropolis; it is to counteract the isolation of the individual in the mass society*" (*Utopian*, p. 151). This continuation of *Communitas* also holds that such planning must be noncoercive and nonbureaucratic, openly done with community involvement, in contrast to our more usual urban planning which also often changes evils by increasing them. While the Goodmans' proposal has some of the usual New Yorker parochialism in assuming the problems and values of that city to be unique, it does seem sensible, though nearly two decades have brought it only slightly closer to realization. While the more amenable city should be everyone's concern, Goodman naively fails to consider it is not really anyone's issue in the pseudopluralistic American technocracy.

Goodman also made utopian-practical responses to other conditions of technocracy. For a January to June stint in 1963, he was a columnist on TV for the *New Republic*. He savaged the media and made some deceptively simple sounding proposals for reform. For example, in "Television: The Continuing Disaster,"[60] he shrewdly noted that the main subjects of the medium are "the formats, rituals and personalities" of the medium itself (p. 99), though he does not further explore the means and effects of the institutional narcissism. "Although TV pretends to be a medium of news, information, and entertainment, it programs in terms of its own image and a putative audience response" (p. 102) in an endless cycle of insular ritualism for a passive audience under top-down corporate control. He counters that the society should "break up the networks by a complete new deal in the franchises, and decentralize control" (p. 103). For with "many hundreds of centers of responsibility and initiative, there will occur many opportunities for direct local audience demand and participation, and for the honest and inventive to get a hearing and try to win their way." But that is doubtful unless quite different people—and structures—take control. Business, the usual institutional hierarchies, "professionalism," and much else would also have to be eliminated for real broadcast difference. Perhaps Goodman sensed this before quickly fleeing the field.

In an article more than a decade earlier on "Popular Culture,"[61] Goodman had argued that "the American popular arts provide a continual petty draining off of the tensions nearest the surface" (p. 81), and compared them to chewing gum to satisfy deep oral needs. Further debasement comes from the "proprietary control of the media by the tribe of intermediary bureaucrats" (p. 86). His modest counterproposal then was to ignore the popular arts and concentrate on little theater and other autonomous artistic efforts.

As a writer, of sorts, for little theaters Goodman also responded with a number of pieces around their problems: how culturally to "live and breathe creatively in a society whose technology and organizations unavoidably make for conformity" (p. 116). He had various proposals for artistic autonomy.[62] To encourage "a free, rather than a mass, democracy" requires "a countervailing force of independent and dissenting media of all kinds" (p. 127). One device would be to tax commercial media to support dissenting media; thus it would "structurally generate its own antidote" (p. 139). No doubt that approach has some merit (in contrast to most of what is done by the National Endowments for Arts and Humanities), though probably not much political feasibility.[63] But perhaps we should also question Goodman's seriousness in that he seemed to find no merit in the countervailings of the "counterculture" of the late 1960s.[64] Perhaps Paul Goodman's sense of American culture was too alienated from the actual minority as well as majority streams to be very pertinent.

His libertarian emphasis appeared fairly constant, if a bit askew at times, in these various proposals. This applies to several anticensorship proposals also, as in "Pornography and the Sexual Revolution" written in the early 1960s when literary censorship generally came to a judicial end in America. He argues against all sexual censorship. But he tiresomely quibbles with the inevitable American legal mode of case-precedent—the *Ulysses*, Roth, and *Lady Chatterley* decisions—perhaps out of ignorance. The comments on Lawrence's novel suggest a vulgar misreading—"neurotic fantasy of a frigid woman and a class-resentful 'dominating' man" (p. 88). But Goodman never had much literary perception, and compulsively knocked his literary betters. He isn't against eroticism, "since sex is a jolly subject" (p. 92) and "sexual action is a proper action of art." Nonartistic pornography, he asserts, serves masturbation. But he doesn't go into the Enlightenment (and Constitutional) issue of "freedom of speech" belonging to a separate order from other free actions, a fiction which raises perplexities and which partly allows, by legal casuistry, that which the majority society otherwise disapproves. Yet his superficial arguments serve a good end: legislating morality not only doesn't work but helps cause the very damage—pornographic fascination—which it seeks to control.[65] "When excellent human power [sexuality] is inhibited and condemned, it will reappear ugly and dangerous" (p. 93). If there were no censorship, and even "hard-core pornography" was allowed on the mass media, sex would be brought into fuller relation with other values. That would also help remove the greatest "curse of censorship," the production of "too many and too trivial art works, all of them inhibitedly pornographic" (p. 97). As for the sadomasochism which pervades our culture—from guilt, from mores in transition, and from the separating out of sex from other experiences— it might be reduced by integrating "sexual expression with other ordinary or esteemed activities of life" and, therefore, "must diminish the need to combine sex with punishment and degradation" (p. 98). Goodman's psychological perceptions here may be a lot better than his literary, legal, and philosophical ones. However, he seems to have confused a limited symptom, overt censorship, with larger causes, such as patterns of social control, and quite ignored the systematic precensorship and processing which constitute most of the real censoring means in this society. As one who has been engaged in many censorship disputes, I find bits of Goodman's argument plausible—and agree that sexual censorship should be abolished—but I also find much of his discussion arrogantly superficial.

That, I am sorry to say, must also be said for many of his "practical proposals," whether for "shoe-string" inventiveness as supposed alternative to "Big Science," or for morally purifying otherwise unchanged technology (the pathology of "space exploration," nuclear energy, etc.), or dispersing broadcast media to what would most likely be local-power structures and bigots, or changing traffic, sex, education, culture, without much attempt to understand why the controls exist or what larger conditions must also be changed. Yet I suspect one might well find a defense for the social functions of his often mediocre thinking in his utopian-practical gestures. While the short-circuited proposals may not really be applicable, thinking about the banning of cars, the reducing of technological scale, the elimination of censorship, the returning to direct arts, and his other "proposals," may encourage fuller awareness. In his self-defense (in *Utopian*), Goodman thinks of his gestures as "risky" in shortcutting usual processes and bringing out diguised conflicts—though certainly our technocracy and its weird culture may be far more extreme and dangerous. The surfaced conflicts may be therapeutic in disrupting people's set acceptance and stupidity, "for stupidity is a character defense" (p. 22). That is optimistic but perhaps sometimes true. Foolish proposals (though he was incapable of admitting that they were) may be clinically necessary for the society and lead to something larger: "In our era, to combat the emptiness of technological life, we have to think of a new form, the conflictful community" (p. 22). That may be a therapy for restoring vitality. And if that be the gadfly function, we might well agree, and even go along with many of Goodman's obvious but teasing inadequacies.

V *Psyching Society*

Much of Goodman's criticism displays an insistent psychologizing. Yet, as his fictions reveal, he had little sense of subtlety of individual psychology and mostly perceived persons in terms of stock situations and types. As with many people, his psychoanalytic emphasis seemed to be a mode of aggression. He apparrently read Freud in the 1930s—not surprising in his New York Jewish intellectual ambience—and seems to have found some self-confirmation for his literary role-playing in other writers of the psychoanalytic movement, such as Otto Rank (*Art and the Artist*).[66] Since his vanguardist and sexual identifications did not incline him to a Marxian faith, Freudianism provided the theories and metaphors that served as ideological weapons. Psychotherapeutics less provided personal insight than categories for fending off the alien world. Those were given a radical twist in the middle-1940s, concurrent with Goodman's turn to libertarianism, by the simplistic revolutionary sexual theories of the ex-Freudian and ex-Marxist—and rather "mad scientist" experimenter—Wilhelm Reich. Thus Goodman became one of the first influential American psychoanalytic radicals, or left-Freudians, long before Norman Mailer, Herbert Marcuse, Norman D. Brown, and others.[67] It was a striking role.

"The Political Meaning of Some Recent Revisions of Freud," (in *Nature*) retains some historical interest for posing the position. This polemic against what were called the neo-Freudians—Karen Horney, Erich Fromm (and more briefly the less liberal Franz Alexander)—emphasizes their rejection of the importance of the "instinctual life" (p. 47) and their considerable acceptance of the arbitrary authority of our social ordering (p. 50). Reich's revolutionary views provided the contrasting revision of Freud in insisting on "general sex-liberation in education, morals, and marriage" (p. 55), with further implications for the broad freeing of character and society. Sexual repression is *"the direct cause of the submissiveness of the people to present political rule of whatever kind"* (p. 56). Goodman assumes here of course, the

anarchist premise that all political submission is wrong, where the
liberal revisionists allowed that there were good and bad sub-
missions. While agreeing with Reich's demands for a sexual
"revolution in morals and economy, perhaps especially with
regard to adolescence," Goodman does parenthetically acknowl-
edge the inadequacy of Reich's "excessively simple and Rousseau-
ian" (p. 57) views, but he insists they will do for now as "the
psychology of the revolution" (p. 58).[68] Some such "pragmatics"
of social and political choices tended to be determining for most
of Goodman's theories.[69]

His interest in Reichean psychology as well as his personal
problems led him into therapy with an American Reichean
(Alexander Lowen) and into related psychological theory, then
to another therapist (Lore Perls) and into a paid job developing
a related therapeutics into a book (with Fritz Perls), and finally
into paid practice as a "lay analyst" for about a decade.[70] The
book, volume two of *Gestalt Therapy* (1951), seems mostly to
be by Goodman, though from suggestions of Fritz Perls and the
influence of his therapist-teacher-friend Lore Perls, and Ralph
Hefferline (who did volume one, a therapeutic technology of
exercises for self-awareness, on which I'll not further comment).
It is Goodman's most ambitious effort at theorizing. The subtitle, "Excitement and Growth in the Human Personality," might
seem more pertinent than the title for this forerunner of what
was to be known in the 1960s as "humanistic" or "encounter"
psychiatry. The term "gestalt" for pattern was borrowed from
a rather different psychological experimentation going back to
the 1920s (Köehler, Goldstein) on the structure of perception.
Goodman takes over some of the earlier gestalt terminology—
"background/figure," "wholes of experience," "unified structures"
—as organizing metaphors for a modified Freud-cum-Reich emphasis on biological responses and his and Perls' insistence on
the immediate sociocultural context of neurotic problems (pp.
227 ff.). Antiscientism provides some of the cutting edginess.[66] The
modern epidemic conviction that most or even all of reality is
neutral is a sign of the inhibition of spontaneous pleasure, play-
fulness, anger, indignation, and fear (an inhibition caused by
such social and sexual conditioning as create the academic
personality)" (p. 233). That libertarian scoring-off also directs

us to the problems of "the neurosis of normalcy" (p. 237) and the therapeutic direction of encouraging the "creative" efforts of the patient to confront and change his reality instead of acquiesing to it. For this, mentalist psychologies are an avoidance of the issue; gestalt experimentation is "irrelevant" to the pressing human problems"—so are other scientistic psychologies, including "the rather dry and affectless syndrome of the positivist disease" (p. 268); and the nonsocial concern of conventional psychoanalysis falsifies experience (p. 240). Obviously what Goodman pursues is a tendentious libertarian *social* psychology.

Much of the work is tiresomely and defeatingly jargonish, overgeneralized, and theologically abstract—even relative to a field notorious for such obfuscation—and quite lacks concrete cases, clinical detail, and human specificity.[71] Anarchistic assertions provide its most striking points. Therapy should less cure the sick than provide a Socratic education into a new concept of virtue, which for Goodman is "happiness," but "our standard of happiness is too low, it is contemptibly too low; one is ashamed of our humanity" (p. 248) for it. So one less seeks to cure the individual—"it is impossible for anyone to be extremely happy until we are happy more generally" (p. 251)—than to get him busy with the "creative possibility" of curing the society. This, of course, must be conventionally disruptive since "the average way of life" is "pathological" (p. 311). And "far from being able to take fitness to social institutions as a rough norm, a doctor has more hope of bringing about the self-developing integration of a patient if the patient learns to adjust his environment to himself than if he tries to learn to maladjust himself to society" (p. 309, also p. 334).

In this libertarian defiance and the attack on the "adjustment ethic" and the "psychology of subordination," as Reichean sociologist Don Calhoun labeled the prevalent theories of the time, Goodman argues not for getting rid of a patient's conflicts but for heightening awareness of them, even creating a "crisis" (p. 356), for "neurosis is the premature pacification of conflicts" (p. 360) and the conceited "resignation" to them (p. 364). So Goodman repeatedly slashes at the Stoic-cum-Protestant morality so antipathetic to him—the "stoic apathy" (p. 271), the lonely willed affectlessness (p. 464).[72] No stiff upper lip for Goodman.

Apparently drawing on Reich's notions of "body armouring" in his *Character Analysis* (and on some of Lowen's therapeutic applications), Goodman views stiffness in posture and breathing as specific indicators of neurotic resignation, as are also withholding tears, sexual cries and orgasm. Strict cleanliness, decorum, and niceness, even unwillingness to sit on floors or generally sprawl out (as he informed me at the time), or most of what might be indicated by "letting go," provide further symptoms. His therapeutic arguments aim, a bit paradoxically, to correct what has usually been called "self-discipline."[73] Sex and other physicality, appetite generally, should not be restricted: "If these things are let be, they will spontaneously regulate themselves, and if they have been deranged they will tend to right themselves" (p. 247). For "the extent to which we agree to situations in which self-regulation rarely operates, to that extent we must be content to live with diminished energy and brightness" (p. 275). In his earlier libertarian writings he called this the "natural"; in the jargon in *Gestalt Therapy* it becomes "Organismic Self-Regulation"; or, in a charming leap, "it is nothing but the old device of the Tao, 'stand out of the way.' "

Goodman was also one of the first to make much of what Marcuse and others later developed, the double-bind of American "sexiness," with its apparent permissiveness towards sexuality "accompanied by a decrease in the excitement and depth of the pleasure." Loss of puritan-intensity, as some have argued? No, says Goodman, we should see this "desensitizing as similar in kind to the rest of the desensitizing, contactlessness, affectlessness now epidemic" in our double-binding social order. For "the release of sexuality has come up against a block of what is not released; anxiety is aroused; the acts are performed, but the meaning and feeling is withdrawn. Not fully completed, the acts are repeated. Guiltiness is generated by anxiety and the lack of satisfaction" (p. 337).[74] And that, of course, compounds the obsessive-action-dissatisfaction pattern into compulsive titillation, seduction, and the rest. One consequence is punitive sexuality—"the dream of American love is sado-masochistic" (p. 347)—while another is pseudo-acceptance: "A chief social device for isolating sexuality is, paradoxically, the healthful, sane, scientific attitude of sex-education on the part of educators and progressive parents" (p. 337). This reductively sterilizes sex: "the so-called wholesome attitude, that turns an act of life into a practice of hygiene, is a means of control and compartmenting" (p. 338), analogous to our other pseudoliberal, one-dimensionalizing, permissively camouflaged dominations.

A similar astute insight, I think, comes out in Goodman's view of aggression; "the inhibition of aggression" he sees as a "chief block" to emotional fullness (p. 337). (Now monumented, I suppose, in the pervasively compulsive "Have a nice day.") Limited "aggression is the 'step toward' the object of appetite or hostility" (p. 342), and is therefore not to be rejected; "inhibiting the aggressions does not eradicate them but turns them against the self," for "without aggression, love stagnates and becomes contactless" (p. 345). While Goodman's discussion here lacks specifics, it seems clear from other writings that he wants strong disagreement, verbal argument and attack, a broad sense of ungoing conflict, even sometimes a salutary fistfight, as open expressiveness.[75] Such a view assumes that local and direct aggressions provide releasing antithesis to the submerged, generalized and more destructive aggressions. I agree (as did Blake, with "Opposition is true friendship."), though the argument needs more discrimination and development, including its relation to the paradoxical insight that the "most salient passional characteristics of our epoch are violence and tameness" (p. 339).

Along with the fuller release of immediately responsive sex and aggression goes "regression." Attacking Freudian notions of libidinal chronology, just as he had rejected Freudian treatment of unfolding the history of a trauma, Goodman holds that the stock adjustment verbalism of 'infantile/mature" (p. 291) misleads since "*no* persisting desire can be regarded as infantile or illusory" (p. 296). "*The childish feelings are important, not as a past that must be undone but as some of the most beautiful powers of adult life that must be recovered . . .*" (p. 297). Some of the conditions that we think of as "childish," such as impatience for gratification or free-floating fantasy (p. 302), he analyzes as positive, while the adult restraint or repression of them serves neurosis.[76] This tough-minded Rousseauism urges us to recapture childhood, not as remembrance or idealization but as positive

acceptance of regressive desires and, I suspect, enjoying what
Freud called the "polymorphously perverse."

In large part, Goodman was no Freudian: denying the
chronology of maturity and accepting the infantile into adult
life; rejecting (though sometimes inconsistently) much of repression, sublimation,[77] the historical etiology of the neurosis—
and thus the domination of the "unconscious" as well as the
"talking cure." Freud he saw as obsessively verbal in approach,
insufficiently emphasizing physical neurosis, the psychosomatic,
bio-therapy, and the like. Goodman moved in other, more volun-
taristic, phenomenological and libertarian, directions. He also
rejected Freud's Thanatos; the "death instinct" was not inherent
in the organism but only in its defeat (p. 349 ff.)—an unimpressive
optimism. He also rejected part of Freud's theory of innate human
aggression, substituting in part the frustration-aggression hypothesis of American ameliorist psychology. Thus Goodman
eliminated the tragic conflict between the instincts and the social
order, I believe, that Freud posited in *Civilization and Its Dis-
contents*. Goodman apparently insisted in therapy as in theory on
sticking closer to what he took to be the instinctual life, including
homosexuality. *His* Freud partly intended sexual freedom but
the "history of psychoanalysis itself is a study of how teeth are
drawn by respectability. It is a perfect illustration of Max Weber's
law of the Bureaucratization of the Prophetic" (p. 339). Except,
of course—as we learn somewhat ambiguously from some of
Goodman's other essays around Freud—the charismatic leader
connived in his own neutered institutionalization by the movement he fathered. While Gestalt Therapy was much involved in,
and dependent on, psychoanalysis, it defiantly deviated far from
the main tradition.[78]

It is certainly also deviant in another sense as a psychological
theory in its lack of gender awareness—I recall no mention of
women or of any sexual differentiation in the entire book—which,
in a theory supposedly insisting on instinctual behavior and its
social context, seems peculiar indeed. Nor was there much more
than passing mention of productive behavior, such as work and
vocation (as on p. 316), which would seem essential to the theory's
social concern.

Goodman's treatment of art also tends away from the psychoanalytic emphasis on dream and sublimation of neurosis to concern for "the concentrated sensation and in the playful manipulation of the material medium" (p. 245). Indeed, he takes art as one of the most positive forms of therapy—even literature: "linguistic reform—the cure of empty symbols and verbalizing—is possible only by learning the structure of poetry and humane letters, and finally by making poetry and the common speech poetic" (p. 332).[79] Furthermore, the lack of responsiveness, passion, creative activity *is* the illness, and "the appalling incuriosity of people is an epidemic and neurotic symptom" (p. 330).

Our society originates most of the illness for this specifically political psychotherapy: "Our social problems are usually posed to conceal the real conflicts and prevent the real solutions" (p. 394). We thus live in a world of "chronic low-grade emergency" (p. 278) with problems magnified by an over-size and unmanageable social ordering with its constant false stimulation which leads to emotional nullity and the loss of vitality (p. 347). His answers: "unblocking" the full range of feeling; sexual and other physical freedom and release; spontaneous and creative behavior, including limited aggression and maintaining the infantile; a sustained radical social hostility to the status quo and its institutions and ideologies; and an active engagement with the immediate world on terms of a natural, self-regulating, passion for the fullest direct but not isolated life.

While *Gestalt Therapy* probably gives Goodman's fullest libertarian prescription, some of it may be obscured by the jargon, abstract writing, and insufficient development of a suggestive but hardly first-rate theorizing. While it has little to tell us of subtle, complex interior life, it is peculiarly American—in its optimistic pragmatism, its here-and-now emphasis, its rough and eccentric fervours, and in its intention to psyche-out our society.[80] In his later writings, too, Goodman rarely pursues psychology in other than its social dimensions and as a polemical weapon. For example, in writing on the "psychology" of the Cold War, he views it with extreme broadness as part of the pandemic frustrations of modern social ordering. Thus "inadequate discharge" of hostilities in overstimulated but powerless roles not only inhibits humane responsiveness but produces "primary masochism" (Reich) and the desire for suicidal violence, "by a wish

for the catastrophe which they [most Americans] rationally oppose." Personal gratification, then, rather than other political
considerations provide the issues. "An occasional fist fight, a
better orgasm, friendly games, a job of useful work, initiating
enterprizes, deciding real issues in manageable meetings, and
being moved by things that are beautiful, curious, or wonderful—
these diminish the spirit of war because they attach people to
life."[81] While an admirable credo, this *ad hominem* ignoring of
collective motivations and authorities may provide only a distant
counter to the social psychology of the specific pathologies of
Cold War militarism.

The rather gross side of this psychologizing appears in Goodman's responses to individuals, which may perhaps be epitomized
in the verse, "If you had had a better fuck last night, / you would
not now be guilty."[82] However, he of course also recognizes more
general conditions. In "The Psychology of Being Powerless" (in
Province) he puts emphasis upon the dominance of anomie
(Durkheim), the usual disease attributed to urban breakdown,
but instead of applying it to the marginal, and the like, he savages
the suburban middle class. They are more dangerous than mere
paranoid bigots because "middle-class squeamishness and anxiety,
a kind of obsessional neurosis, are a much more important cause
of segregation than classical race prejudice" (p. 108). Middle-
class fears are pervasive because they identify "with the efficient
system itself, which is what renders *them* powerless" and makes
such resentfully the "most dangerous group of all" (p. 117).
Perhaps so, though the indictment seems rather too loose and
broad to be satisfactory.

A couple of years later, in another ragged foray into social
psychologizing, "Reflections on Racism, Spite, Guilt and Non-
Violence" (1968; reprinted in *Nature*), Goodman more shrewdly
emphasized the 'indifference" of middle-class whites to blacks;
blacks, of course, are not in a position to be indifferent to whites,
and so *their* responses tend to be "racist." While Goodman also
notes some of the paradoxical American attitudes around race—
populism and prejudice, generosity and anxiety—he shows little
awareness of the mythic levels of racism, such as one might
recognize in Faulkner. Like most libertarians, he suspects "black
power" and separationist demands "because in fact the unity of

mankind is the truth." He affirms the tradition of nonviolent protest and hopes it will lead to "opening areas of freedom piecemeal"—the ameliorist emphasis of his later years—but this appears in a somewhat forlorn context since we need "profound institutional changes" which amount to something near a "religious conversion." Such views hardly require a psychological theory, just perplexed responsiveness and his version of libertarianism. Goodman's psyching of American society, then, was yet another literary role, though one partly salutary in suggestively emphasizing the social impositions upon a full sense of life.

VI *Protest Politics*

As my summary discussion of Goodman's therapeutic writings should indicate, his social psychologizing both arose from protest against dominant American society and turned back at it in protest and even anti-protest. In a broad sense, protest shapes most of his roles and his writings. But here I want to briefly consider his protesting roles in a more limited, political, sense. He was intermittently and earnestly involved in manifestos of dissent, demonstrations, leafleting, picketing, marches, calls for resistance, displays of civil disobedience, and other symbolic gestures of defiance of the State for nearly three decades: from a mild call for "evasion" of military conscription in 1942—"not to cooperate" and employ "cunning, fraud, or flight as will best serve"—through picketing of a federal prison for release of Conscientious Objectors after World War II, then, after a gap, to opposition to the reinstituted military draft in the late 1940s;[83] a gap again of some years, and he could be found protesting nuclear war policy ("bomb shelters" and "testing"), which merged into the "Worldwide General Strike for Peace" in the early 1960s and its picketing and other demonstrations;[84] participating in some actions of campus rebels in the mid-1960s; joining in many actions against the American Vietnam War (teach-ins, street marches, and so on); and encouraging draft and tax resistance in the later 1960s. Honorable causes, all. Furthermore, in the mid-1960s he was often viewed, by both admirers and despisers, as "the foremost tribune of our youthful counter culture" in its rebellions.[85]

However, if that should suggest an image of Goodman as a really "militant" radical, anarcho-pacifist leader, or tough "activist," it would be misleading. He was apparently never fired, beaten, jailed, prosecuted, or otherwise made to suffer for his dissent; I have been told by a knowing militant that Goodman's roles in conceiving, organizing, and leading protests were usually peripheral. He was often viewed, as he insisted, as a "literary man." Temperamentally Goodman was not brave or militant, and there was little of the rebel or martyr or revolutionary about him. Goodman was for a decade or so involved with an active group of left-pacifists—David Dellinger, Staughton Lynd, David McReynolds, A. J. Muste, and others around *Liberation*.[86] Yet, it seems to me, there was something a bit condescending in his attitude toward Civil Disobedience movements. Certainly he was skeptical about most ways of overt defiance, preferring "devious and flexible" noncooperation and "alternative" modes of resistance. He feared the politics and style of any massive protest.[87] Though he never much developed the view, he seems to have held, as some other libertarians have, to styles of "subversion," that is, covert noncooperation, Schweikism, avoidance, bohemian deviance, privateering, nonallegiance—the antipolitics of the individualist "opting out" of the repressive system. More to his taste than overt resistance was the belief that personal and communal liberation—the sexual and vocational and autonomous small-group activities—importantly transformed the dominating order simply by existing. There are contradictions here in an earnest moralist looking, somewhat uncertainly, toward ironic dissidence.

As a writer, of course, Goodman felt that some of his statements were themselves acts of dissent and protest. And sometimes they may be so viewed. In one of his better-written articles, "The Devolution of Democracy" (1962),[88] he places the pseudoliberal Kennedy administration in the line of decline of American democracy, for "power and inertia have boldly filled up the vacuum" left by the corrupting of liberties and the dwindling of early Jeffersonian promises. Kennedyism showed the "*image* of government, active persons with no idea." By refusing to question the basic premises of the baroque warfare state, and Cold War World, no extension of liberties, and therefore no maintenance of freedom, was possible. The Kennedy administration had revealed itself as a political form of hipsterism: "It is the cool and activist role-playing of vitality in a situation of impotence" (p. 10). Goodman illustrates, with applied literary criticism, the Kennedy-style jargon of playing "tough" and the dangerous "posturing," along with the fatuousness of the trimmer-intellectuals sucking on such power politics and their hollow claims for some ameliorist milk. More radically than in his own later statements, Goodman says, "If the aim is *merely* to mitigate, and not attack the structure and causes of the evil, one will not *even* mitigate" (p. 7). If the warlike premises and the cosmetic politics continue, the end will be "a kind of fascism of the majority" (p. 21). Needed: *"action outside of their politics, by every means and on every relevant issue"* (p. 22). This was prescient, both about the administration that would end, logically enough, in a massively futile war in Southeast Asia and about the protest politics then developing in the Bay area and the Civil Rights movement, which would be so important in the next decade.

Goodman seems to have been stimulated to his best efforts in attacking typical American "liberalism." So, too, with the good piece titled "The Ineffectuality of Some Intelligent People" (in *Drawing the Line*) where he makes some incisive points about the inabilities of many of the educated to act out their convictions. Anxious conventionality leads some to play the established game even when they know that the rules are "manipulated against them" (p. 98). They often combine a pathetic lust for status and self-importance with a futile hope of "influencing" what they know to be wrong and bad. We have as a society few traditions of public honor in which officials—or academics—resign over principle. Add to this a self-deluding "realism" and therefore inability to recognize change, and the "respectability" which makes some decent people fear a breach of manners or taste more than a violation of sense or conscience. Educated decency is thus little force for social change.

Rightly enough, Goodman savages academics. Professors seem prone to insulate understanding from action (that American neutered concept of "academic freedom") and commit themselves to merely "verbalized" values generally in politics, and even on educational issues. Social scientists especially deserve condemnation for the "pathology of the present social scientific method" (p. 104), with its detached scientistic pretenses, its inadequate views of human nature and community, and its failure to recognize moral action as a crucial part of identity and relationship. Never having had a regular place in an institutional order, Goodman probably undervalues the motives of "security" for many—a "secondary motive" (p. 105) to other satisfactions—but rightly sees it as often illusory. He notes that the fashionable concern with "decision-making" is itself a symptom of fear and powerlessness. The failure of the educated-decent to act against war and militarism and other patent evils also expresses their lack of "psychosexual and communal" responsiveness (p. 110) as well as a lack of deep democratic conviction. True enough. Yet, as his own periods of quietism, as in the 1950s, showed—and as many of the radical discovered again in the 1970s—public action and political protest are not just moral choices but subject to the ambience and the desperate-receptive temper of time and place. There is a sense, we might almost say, of even radical decorum. History exists, and it was Goodmanian foolishness to ignore it.

Among the many speeches on campuses and at conferences and rallies (on education, war, decentralizing, and similar issues) by Goodman, perhaps that which attracted the most attention was "A Causerie at the Military-Industrial" (1967), presented to the National Security Industrial Association in Washington (and reprinted in *Line*, with descriptions and the response included). For the reader of Goodman, the polemics seem usual and not strikingly put: the misuse of technology for militarism and for destructive urbanization, with the vicious circularity of corporate Research and Development; the desperate need in a society "that is cluttered, overcentralized, and overadministered" for "simplification, and decontrol"; and the insistence on "moral criteria" for the applications of technology, planning, and power. The tone was indignant and moralistic, and most of the immediate response of the corporate and other officials was negative— a proper compliment.

When, in the same period, Goodman spoke or wrote for his Movement peers, as in "The Duty of Professionals,"[89] his position showed rather more ambiguity. It claimed a pluralistic dissent wending its way among moralistic purism, revolutionary extremism, and liberal reluctance, with a quaint twist into professionalist guild ethics. As an anarcho-pacifist (in contrast with religious pacifists), Goodman did not hold to absolute nonviolence; some violence was appearing in the mass protest actions; his comment: "Morally, in my opinion, this sporadic violence is neither right nor wrong, though sad" (p. 167). Obviously, some of it was engendered by the authorities. That engendered by revolutionism, by "those who want disorder for its own sake as part of a theory of general (world) breakdown and insurrection" (p. 168), lacked discrimination and other sense. But "as a populist" he would exclude no one. Most desirable for Goodman would be conflict kept to therapeutic levels—apparently that sometimes includes limited coercion and aggression—defined by "what we want to live with if we win" (p. 169). The proper ethic here would be one of suitable means to libertarian ends.

We can, he suggests, "distinguish three kinds of necessary resistance": mass protest demonstrations; accepted legal protest (courts, petitioning, and the like); and "professional resistance" (p. 169). Oddly, he ignores several other ways of resisting, such as exemplary "witness" and certain styles of "subversion," but this just may be his frequent careless thinking and writing. Or it may also be reformist conservativism. For while Goodman defends some variety of resistance—mass advertising (used by some antiwar groups in the mid-1960s), petition and lobbying, draft refusal (and its support by others)—he emphasizes "professional" ethics. By this he does *not* mean socially conscious radicalism—the "politicalization" of professionals encouraged by some leftists at the time—but an emphasis on standards within specialties by doctors, architects, technologists, and the like. Goodman may have correctly recognized a developing move to somewhat greater guild responsibility, and I have the sense that there has been a little such professional reform in the decade since he wrote.

In political theory, such views as Goodman's here provide an ameliorist version of the somewhat desperate leftist search for a "new class" as agent of social change in place of the now generally conservative industrial proletariat—one with more continuity than the often erratic and atomizing *lumpen* dissidents

(students and other marginals) and with more purpose than
the generally coopted reformism of the liberal-bourgeoisie. But
I think the focusing on "professionals" as a social-moral force is
conservative, if not worse. As with Lenin's raising up of administrative "cadres," or even Veblen with "engineers," we may get
a new class with a dominating vengeance. That those who run
much of the social machinery should do so with high moral
purpose and responsibility seems an obvious decency, but it hits
against the realities that their mechanisms have other ends. The
professions, of course, are structured for certification and other
controlled access; they are dominated by hierarchical roles and
elitist advantages and crude profiteering; above all, they serve
self-rationalizing and self-perpetuating ends. Organized doctors
and technologists and academics can try to "maintain standards"
in their controls of others but they certainly will not encourage
freedom (especially from them) or equality (especially with
them). In the long run, professional groupings resist or under-
mine most libertarian changes, as they must, and a good society
must deprofessionalize.[90]

Goodman's lack of theoretical concern with his exaltation of
renewed guild morality makes his claims merely sentimental.
His identification, in his last years, with professional morality
is more curious than serious. He ends his last book of social
criticism, *New Reformation*, with a personal note: "I am pleased
to notice how again and again in this book I have returned to
the freedoms, duties, and opportunities of earnest professionals.
It means that I am thinking from where I breathe."[91] What a
pathetic delusion! For Goodman was an *outré* literary man most
of his life; he was less involved in a profession than an escape
from one (as he had admitted). He certainly had little experience with guild effort, carefully disciplined social functioning,
or even a regular income. To pretend that American intellectual
writers as a group have some sort of professional community
and ethic is a bad joke. (Even their coteries don't endure well,
fortunately.) The *virtu* of the Man of Letters is, as with saint-
liness, that it is unhoused, pure professing. Indeed, Goodman for
years had made much of just such special freedom of the literary
radical. Being a Man of Letters may, somewhat uncomfortably,
be joined with a profession (teaching, media, and the like), but

it is only a sellable expertise in a debased way. Goodman's other occupations than Man of Letters (his purposive activities and ways of making a living)—for a decade a marginal psychotherapist; for another decade a well paid dissident lecturer and publicist—hardly constitute, in the sense he means, a "profession." His earnest literary role-playing—and perhaps a clichéd social ambition out of his lower middle-class Jewish background—had betrayed him into inconsistent and downright false gestures which also deny his antischooling views. By the late 1960s Goodman wanted a way out of the dilemmas of protest politics, a choice other than that of affirming a madly devolving power system—with its tendencies to "expand meaninglessly for its own sake" and "to exclude human beings as useless"[92]—or its simple destructive inversion in revolutionism. Knowing similar officials and militants, I can partly sympathize with his revulsions. But his latching on, and even earnestly identifying with, the smug moralisms of controlling specialist elites, in a search for the politics of "the finite," was hardly admirable. To quaintly emphasize guild manners, whatever the decent impetus, reinforces the conservative institutional powers of specialism and special privilege and is far, indeed, from protest, reformation, or social liberation. Goodman's protest against protest—it is hardly more serious than that—defeated some of his role as a therapeutic gadfly. But perhaps it can also be provocatively therapeutic to truly perceive Paul Goodman's failures.

CHAPTER 4

The Literary Hobbyist

ON their merits, there would be little sense in discussing most of Paul Goodman's half dozen published novels, four collections labeled "stories,". eighteen published plays, and half-dozen volumes of verse. Pathetically, they are often quite literally incompetent—marked by trite and mangled language, bumblingly inconsistent manners and tones, garbled syntax and forms, embarrassing pretentiousness and self-lugubriousness, and pervasive awkward writing. Some of this—the pedantry, mawkishness, jargon, carelessness—may be explained biographically, but some—the woodenness, the misused slang, the bad modifiers and parallelism, the metaphoric flatness—seems beyond explanation. His "literary" works were often so bad as to cast doubt on all his writing and thinking. Still, some commentators take Goodman's literary debris seriously, perhaps out of kindly personal and political motives, so some discussion of these twenty volumes seems necessary. With apologies for bothering with the bad, I will try to summarize them and kindly emphasize curious bits and suggestive gestures, without forgetting that most of Goodman's "art" is the hardly readable waste from inappropriate literary role-playing.

Perhaps the most positive way to view Goodman's literary efforts would be to see them as the products of hobbyism—a diversion from his more interesting roles as libertarian social critic.[1] As I have discussed earlier, he took up self-indulgent art activity as an arbitrary substitute for a career, as compensation for what he thought of as an unhappy alienated youth, and as role-justification for his bohemian-bisexual dissident ways. By a remarkable persistence, not least notable for its critical obtuseness, he managed, with the help of friends, subsidized presses, his eventual reputation as a social critic, and earnest *chutzpah,* to publish and republish most of his literary efforts.

106

People do take their hobbies with inordinate seriousness, and Goodman more than most. But even as literary hobbyist he kept switching genres, and forms and manners within them, with an indiscriminateness that suggests he could not find a suitable avocation, much less a true *métier*. While he gained little wisdom from persisting in his literary folly and his later writing is often worse than his juvenilia, the debris may be screened for some symptoms of biographical, historical, and other significance among the literary play and pathology.

I *The Imperial Conceit*

Probably Goodman's most ambitious hobbyist project over many years was writing *The Empire City* (1959), ostensibly a four-volume novel including *The Grand Piano* (originally published 1942), *The State of Nature* (1946), *The Dead of Spring* (1950), and *The Holy Terror* (mostly written in 1953, with a section added in 1957, though not published prior to the collection).[2] Rather pathetically, Goodman seems to have thought of it as his masterwork which would become a "classic," a major "picaresque" tale or "comic epic."[3] While more or less admitting that it lacked dramatization, character development, consistent focus and tone, etc., he repeatedly rationalized these inadequacies into positive attributes of his ideological allegory. It makes more sense to see the work as pieces of "cartoon" strips, an odd anthology of sociological and theological ruminations, and as muddled pastiche. One stiltedly announced purpose: "To fashion in our lovely English tongue a somewhat livelier world, I am writing this book" (p. 554). But the writing is hardly readable in its synthetic mixture of pedantry and colloquialism, and there is little realized world, or counterworld.

To summarize coherently would give *The Empire City* more than its due. But to be generous, I suggest first looking at one of the better sections ("Horatio Furioso" of *The Holy Terror*) where the intermittent protagonist, a puppet-caricature called Horatio Alger, goes mad:

Like that fellow in Prague who awoke one morning to find himself transformed into a monstrous bug, so Horatio awoke one morning

and he was for the General for president. He believed in the world of
the *Herald Tribune* and he began to follow the folkways of the
Americans. In a haze of insane clarity, it struck him that the election
of the General would make a (beneficial) difference to our happiness;
and he got out of bed at once, giving his sleeping wife a sentimental
lustless peck on the cheek. He prepared some odorless coffee with a
powder, and sat down with his *Herald Tribune*.

Now when I say he "believed in" the world of that excellent
journal, I don't mean that he embraced the explicit opinions of the
editors and advertisers (nobody is that crazy), but that he took for
granted that what was printed there as the news was indeed the
news, and that the assumptions on which the articles were based was
indeed the way of the world. What a world was that! (p. 502)

While the coy reference to Kafka's "The Metamorphosis," such
redundancy as "sentimental lustless peck," and the final awkward
sarcasm, weaken the passage, it exemplifies the book's most concrete and felicitous style. The writing soon falters, but the theme
is developed at some length.The episode is puzzlingly placed in
January 1953 (apparently also the time of writing),[4] though
the election took place the previous November. Is this Goodman's frequent carelessness, or an arch finger at the reader? The
curious rage at Eisenhower, when that blandly conservative
dullard was probably the least dangerous American president
in the past generation, seems odd since anarchists usually prefer
authorities to be dumb *status quo* idols. But Goodman may have
been desperately looking for a newspaper-level subject.

There are also some easy mockeries of newspaper items, perhaps the most pertinent an anger at the Humphrey bill for
federal funding of schools—a prescient sense of the accelerated
schooling mania. The author also gives a loose lecture that what
is conventionally taken as "news" consists mostly of ritualized
responses and fantasies. True enough, but Horatio rather than
the news editors requires psychotherapy. This Lowen-type
therapy is presented in thinly jokey fragments around the argument that someone must be *"willing to sacrifice his sanity in
order to beat the general by supporting him"* (p. 516). Supposedly, the embrace of the "marginal" in society will be fatal—
the irony of the self-pitying bohemian.

Horatio goes on to a related second therapist who runs "a

combination cat house and employment agency" (p. 524)—a typical jejune vulgarity. Here Goodman's earnest idea about the difficulty of finding meaningful work in our society gets short-circuited into a bad joke—the advice that Horatio should join the PTA. Such a dose of stupidity should bring a "breakthrough of rage and grief" (p. 528), thus restoring him to emotional sanity. At some length, Goodman makes mild satiric jabs at the PTA's pseudodemocracy and irrelevance. Of course some of his points seem a bit extreme for the conventional context, such as that there should not be sexually separate toilets—"the one point where co-education was essential and made sense, in the carnal knowledge of one another" (p. 539). Children should also be encouraged in immediate small aggressions (apparently instead of delayed and displaced hostilities, which are finally more damaging). And the schooling cages should be opened: "*I move that the PTA petition the Board of Education to make education noncompulsory, so that children can go to school when they feel like it*" (p. 541).

In some awkwardly done farce, Horatio spikes the punch so that the PTAers get noisily drunk. But that was anticlimax, for "Horatio had had it, the social reality, and the world of the *Herald Tribune*, and the Parent Teachers Association. And the result was that he was no longer for the General for president" (p. 544). This relatively autonomous section of the novel, a flat, satiric farce, ends, as do many of the pieces of *The Empire City*, on a maudlin note. Horatio cries on Inauguration Day because "history and folly have robbed him" (p. 547) of his patriotic possibilities by treating his views as alien.

Indeed, that is a recurrent theme and the first novel, *The Grand Piano*, was originally subtitled "Almanac of Alienation" (this subtitle is inexplicably dropped in the later collection, though referred to on page 427), then resubtitled "Before the War" (World War II, probably 1939).[5] The nominal protagonist, Horatio, is eleven (inconsistently, he is thirty-two in the "mad" episode, above, in 1953). At first the kid speaks a made-up muddled street jargon, later dropped for the synthetic mixture of pedantry and colloquialism which most of the characters, and the narrator, usually use. A permanent truant, Horatio has learned to read and philosophize in the streets, an expression

of Goodman's antischooling principle. But not much is shown
about the figure and there is little focused development. Goodman loosely recreates his own family structure: no parents
present for Horatio, a talented older brother—here the musician
Lothair (an excuse for Goodman's ruminations on music)—an
earnest sister, Laura. All are on "the dole." Other caricatures
include Mynheer, a pretentious Dutch sometime-sage, who
marries Emily (announced but not shown as a "columnist"),
daughter of Eliphaz, a pompous philosophical Jewish business-
man who runs his house as a department store and fills note-
books with zeros in a *reductio ad absurdum* of the Marxian
view of the transformation of use values into paper "exchange"
values. Many of the names obviously intend allegorical suggestiveness, in a slopped-out way. Other figures appear in a scene
or two—including Goodman's friends under their own names
(George Dennison) or relabeled (Underwood for the historian
Ben Nelson, lecturing on his specialty, medieval ideas of usury)[6]
—and then disappear. With cute ostentation, there are also Santayana, Keats, Buber, Wordsworth, Paul Goodman (as psychologist), Byron, Otto Rank, Kafka (repeatedly "our friend Franz"),
Nietzsche, e. e. cummings, Paul Klee, Lautremont, Rilke
(often), Mallarmé, Freud (repeatedly), Paul Goodman (as
dramatist), Goethe (a favorite), Kierkegaard, Lewis Carroll,
Marx, Seneca, Paul Goodman (as Kantian philosopher), D. H.
Lawrence, Bishop Butler, Maimonides, Paul Goodman (as poet),
Mandeville, Gide (cited as well as plagarized), Tristan Tzara,
Kropotkin, Hobbes, Chuang-Tzu (again and again), God, Aristotle, Paul Goodman (as lover and sage), and so on. Much of
this mix of pedantry, vanity, and vanguardism serves quaintness,
but most of it just seems compulsive autodidact mannerism.

Some theorizing attempts to give abstract depth to the
mannerisms and the cartoon figures. Much of this relates to
sociological notions of the "marginal," the bohemian *lumpen-*
intellectuals, the people who "live in the loopholes" (p. 39) of
megapolitan society.[7] *The Empire City,* to the degree that it
concerns anything other than the author's obsessions,[8] is attempted parabolic history of a coterie of New York petty bourgeois intelligentsia. The same material is better presented by
other writers, such as Delmore Schwartz. Not only would-be

witticisms seem in-groupish but also the peripheral responses to the larger world. Thus nothing of World War II really appears but there is a mild satire of registering for the draft (pp. 46 ff.). No real economic activity is dramatized but there are vague threats of boycotting a false society of superfluities. The few suggestively rebellious phrases and notions lack development, such as the "Society for the Propagation of Vice" (p. 83), which would bring down the society by aggravating private pleasures beyond public utility.

The Empire City raggedly collects vanguardist gestures, from coy undercutting—a footnote which goes "I am baffled by the meaning of . . ." (p. 87)—through non-sequitur conversations (as later made familiar by Barthelme) and bohemian pathology (as in Gaddis, or as later exploited in Pynchon's "sick crew")—those "in beloved misery of looking for love in the face of self-imposed insurmountable obstacles" (p. 90). There is a parody of a poetry reading (pp. 95 ff.), though without the wit of, say, *The Dream Life of Balso Snell*. There are jokey little bits such as "Joy Scouts" for delinquent Boy Scouts. There is a long, earnest commentary on a Wagner performance (pp. 99 ff.)—perhaps pedantically indebted to Thomas Mann—and pedagogically defiant arguments about the city as a natural school (pp. 120 ff.). The entitling grand piano serves as a bit of surrealist burlesque, a punitive gift from the tycoon Eliphas for the family on welfare, who will use it for a bed and bad jokes. There is also the announcement of, but no development for, "Practical Dada" and the "Manifesto of Bombism" (p. 65). The novel, then, is stuffed with the common metaphors of between-wars vanguardist culture—dadaism, bohemianism, Marxism, surrealism, modernist culture heroes and cultisms—but none sufficiently developed to be enduring curiosities or examples of other than self-indulgent cuteness.[9]

Whereas *The Grand Piano* ends with everything ready to blow up,[10] the second novel, *The State of Nature*, presupposes the war going on, far distantly. Generally, "nature" (as we have seen) serves as the highest of metaphors for Goodman. So Part One, "The Weakness of the Ego," rests on a quote from Freud suggesting that if the "ego remains one with the id" (p. 147), then strength follows. The war marks a culture in which ego and id

have destructively separated, the extreme of the self-alienation
of the first novel (p. 226). Thus we arrive at a Hobbesian "state
of nature," an abrogation of the social compact. Somewhat con-
fusingly, there is also the Taoist religious return to "nature"
(p. 175). Perhaps they fuse in the abstract war ruins in which
the characters return to primitive life, a liberating chaos (p. 259).
Natural freedom also allows one to blow up the unnatural—
factories and Archibald MacLeish (p. 265). A bad natural state
exists when atomized people turn to "their individual resources,"
but—and here is one of Goodman's most crucial assumptions as
libertarian social critic—"they would get together again" because
there "arises in people a hunger for common reason" (pp. 266–
67). If that takes the form of "neolithic mores," it is sure to be
positive, as in the increase of post–World War II permissiveness
so that "boys and girls, no longer sexually deprived, were not so
willing to be submissive to authority or even to reason" (p. 273).
That makes the new generation problematic but also "a barrel of
fun." No one constipates an idea with a cliché faster than
Goodman!

There could be a useful irony around the reversal of "nature"
in the notion of an architect who designs striking buildings
becoming a wartime camouflage expert in hiding the buildings.
But Goodman rather muddles it by not developing the architect,
Laura, so the change is little evident, and by rather hysterically
misconstruing World War II camouflage as getting rid of homes,
schools and churches instead of, in fact, obscuring military-
industrial targets into apparent civilian forms (p. 185 ff.). Similar weakness mars Goodman's deployment of moral metaphors
around William James' famous idea that we require "a moral
equivalent of war" to more benignly answer the aggressive needs
of human nature. Goodman's pompous restatement: *"there would
always be a war until people found a better way to put themselves in jeopardy en masse"* (p. 174). His related motif is that
certain wars are psychologically better than others: *"Best of all
was to fight a drawn out losing fight"* (p. 177), apparently because it would dissipate guilt rather than breed bitterness and
vengeance, contrary to what history often indicates.

Intellectually, Goodman was just playing around. So was his
character Lothair when, after imprisonment as a conscientious

objector, he opens the cages of a zoo to ordain the return to a state of nature. In a childishly written scene which makes the action didactically quaint, a tiger eats Emily's young son (p. 233), which is "ironical" in a world in which State violence makes mere meat of twenty million or more. We are to understand that the tigers at least act naturally in a sense in which the war-mechanisms do not, with their "powerful stimuli and small satisfaction!" (p. 237).

The misproportions of stimuli/satisfaction also provide the guiding notions for the later attack on more subtle forms of caging, the postwar American "Sociolatry":[11] "It is the adjustment of the individual to a social role without releasing any new forces of nature. Everywhere there will be personal and public peace (except among the wild and crazy); nowhere will there be love and community. And millions will fall down in the streets of the Asphyxiation" (p. 277). This is probably *not* an early attack on air-pollution but a suffocation from the lack of a full human nature (Goodman, drawing on Reichean therapy, loves breathing metaphors). It will also be a society with a mass culture "impenetrable by any serious or comic word" (p. 278), or any other emotional authenticity. Some of the polemical prophecies could be suggestive. So could some of the incidental sociological arguments for better city planning—"The lack of a plan is not no plan but a bad plan" (p. 267). But that is better presented by far in *Communitas*, though both may be vitiated by a naive view of historical possibility.

Certainly the fictional presentation is vitiated by quite a crude view of what an imaginative history, the novel, requires. The art of following the fragmentary adventures of our "lumpen aristocrat" includes swallowing some badly told anti-Semitic jokes (p. 149), a sticky play with Yiddish irony, such as "*Goyim Nachus*" (p. 156), the artiness of words printed backwards and upside down (pp. 218, 285), and the repeated private diction of erotic obsession in which street punks are "lads," "manly," even "knightly" (p. 246). But perhaps I can summarize the craft of *The Empire City* with an authorial aside which explains that a contraption in the state of nature is "made, like this chapter, with what they picked up here and there" (p. 270). This aesthetic

schizophrenia (but less shrewdly than, say, with William Bur-
roughs) dominates the work.

The third novel, *The Dead of Spring*, subtitled "After a War,"
centers on the neurotic pathos of the New York bohemians now
that there is less external focus: "The hard problem is this: that
the sensible impulse must come from our vital desire, but we
do not feel our vital desire" (p. 285). He called for emotional
responses such as crying (often announced but little shown) as
"liberating and healthful" (p. 289). These alienated must also
learn to "accept our total loss of paradise" (p. 294) in a society
which is basically "demented" (p. 301). Other answers include
quasi-Taoistic pontificating: *"Diminishing error but remaining
close in the awareness of the impasse of nothing practical, large
increments of love are released that are fermenting in the Fertile
Void"* (p. 288).

One way to release love is to create "A Community of Human
Relations" (characteristic redundancy). This takes the wry but
too sketchy form of a utopian plan which appears to me to be
a left-Freudian variation on Fourier's Phalanstery, with sixty-six
types, such as narcissistic male friend, scapegoat, sexually easy
woman, and so on (p. 309).[12] Slithering between earnestness
and jokiness, the community notion disappears, though Lothair
and Emily supposedly reach the secure love community engen-
ders to produce a child, amusingly named St. Wayward.

A perhaps even more wayward manner of love shows itself in
Goodman's rather clinical commentary on his friends, and cartoon characters. (He was working on, and in, Gestalt Therapy
during part of the writing.) The comments seem spiteful; the
"friends" are viewed as "crippled, maimed" and "poisoned and
sick" (p. 329). Their, and his, "dilemma": "Either to dissent from
the social community and thereby to grow sickly, deformed and
mad—for where else is one to thrive?—or to conform to it and
go mad and stiffle" (p. 330). This terribly anxious view of nonconformity sees the dissenters, self included, as total victims of
"the strangling organization" of society so that they become
"hateful and resentful" (p. 332). As the compulsive metaphors
of strangulation suggest, this is a report on personal anxiety,
not social reality. Not surprisingly, the resolution is a leap into
magical air—"ride the whirlwind like the Master of the Way."

A few years later, in the fourth book of *The Empire City*, Goodman's wind blows different advice. But I want first to glance at some of the intermittent narrative, such as it is, of the third novel. Horatio, too, becomes crippled, blind, for awhile "because there was nothing worth seeing" (p. 336). Oddly, we at last get some physical detailing of the figure, who turns out to be five foot ten and "well hung" (p. 381) and wears (the first clothes I recall) torn blue pants and a red turtle-neck sweater: "He disguised himself as the kind of love hustler known as Rough Trade" (p. 355)—a type Goodman apparently pursued. Without mockery, the hustler is winged Eros and part of a long "urban pastoral romance" (pp. 341–91), if we can blandly assume the imperial slum to be Arcadia. Rosalind, another undeveloped figure (mostly defined as wanting children—Goodman's usual prejudice about women) falls in love with Horatio. But he is brought to trial for treason since as a lifelong truant he has no records. A loose, righteous burlesque, it isn't funny, but is rationalized, I suppose, by the smug statement: "I'm not so sick as to have an American sense of humor . . ." (p. 377). Horatio also provides what I take to be Goodman's rationalization for being an evasive anarchist and never confronting the State (as did some of his pacifist friends) because he has better things to do (not specified) and refuses to accept authority's definitions (pp. 386–87). But all issues quickly disappear as the sweet judge frees Horatio because of his status as a lover boy. We then get, for an anarchist author, a strange summary praise of judges who expound "the accumulated ancient lore of the people, embodied in the common law," though none of this has been shown. With a different kind of silliness, Rosalind and Horatio (after getting married, escorted by "rough trade") end up sucking a Greek matron's breasts. Pseudorealism has turned to pseudoanarchist ideology and dissolved in pseudomyth (perhaps imitating Cocteau). Later, in an equally pressured pretense at community ritual, there is an archly "Memorial Game" of baseball for the "crazy Laura" who had out of general despair committed suicide (pp. 413 ff.).

Other odd bits in *The Dead of Spring* include more obessional descriptions of fires (pp. 38 ff.), the suggestive characterization of American popular culture of the time as an "outpouring of fruitless longing" which "does not want to be satisfied" (p. 373), and several forced attempts to deal with mourning, such as mixing Jewish ritual and a synthetic melange of modernist poetry (pp. 395 ff.). We also see Goodman's imperceptiveness about work (which also mars his later social criticism) in the too-aesthetic view that what is wrong with most jobs is the lack of vocation and pleasantness rather than the lack of freedom and justice (p. 345). Goodman also exalts Lawrence's dictum of following one's "deepest impulse" (p. 374) but without Lawrence's profound sense that to discover one's deepest impulse is most difficult.[13] There might be interesting matter here, but little is novelistically or intellectually well put.

The major section of the fourth novel, *The Holy Terror*, subtitled "Modern Times," has been discussed above. The rest is mostly thin and self-indulgent stuff, heavy on bathos. The announced purpose seems shockingly conservative: "to show how these gifted friends of mine, who were always so dissident but not necessarily protestant, have now become more satisfied with the folkways of our society" (p. 427). Granted, that was a fashionable climate in the "end of ideology" 1950s, but it's going a bit far to insist that "where I commenced by compiling an Almanac of Alienation" (the dropped subtitle) "I am now concluding with a kind of 'Register of Reconciliation.' Well, to be *au courant* has long been a veritable disease with New York intellectuals.

Rather comically, considering his later social criticism, Goodman adds that American "institutions themselves have insensibly been transformed by our truth" (p. 427)—a conceit that perhaps goes with identifying with the fashionable.[14] But the transformations in the novel consist of forced rituals and fantasies. One is a description of a figure who has surprisingly succeeded in San Francisco as a bar singer, a happy husband, and a charity counselor (pp. 569 ff.). This flatly done tale gets heightened by constant interjections, such as "We marvelled. We were stricken dumb" (p. 575)—a telling instead of showing which usually reveals the novelistically ignorant amateur. But the idea that someone from their parochial circle has a reasonable job, an art with an audience, and a pleasant personal relationship, is so intense that all else should be ignored.[15] Such joys provide

"the holy terror" of the title. The literary incompetence underlines the anxious bathos about the commonplace.[16]

Aesthetically dishonest novelists—Herman Hesse is the best-
known case—leap into arbitrary fantasy to resolve their themes.
Goodman jumps into awkward fairytale in which the child St.
Wayward—with "bronze hair" and "dressed in ultraviolet"—
mounts a unicorn from a medieval tapestry in the Cloisters and
flies off to save Ireland by restoring virility to its men. As we
learn in a staggering doggerel-quality imitation ballad, Saint
Patrick outlawed not only snakes but, mistakenly, something that
looked a bit similar—penises. Or was it done by the Irish literary
character? Listening to young and old storytellers, our Wayward
savior (and resentful author) finds them all disgusting liars, so
much so that "his penis shrunk to the size of a pea" (p. 609).
(Does bad metaphor go with envy?) But before restoring the
staff of life to the Irish, which he intends to do in spite of their
history, their liars and their priests, Wayward flies off with a
mythical laddy to Venice.[17] That city provides final images to
Goodman's concern in the novels with urban design. The end
intends to be a Faustian epiphany as Mynheer, suddenly reap-
pearing as sage, views Wayward and Irish friend on the monument and recognizes that St. Mark's is "the most beautiful
square for the concourse of people that has ever been made by
man. And Mynheer called out to them in a mournful voice that
has forever broken my heart, 'Nay, stay! Stay!' but of course they
did not stay" (p. 617).

This supposedly affirms an ideal possibility for New York,
which in *The Holy Terror* Goodman also displayed in a surprisingly literal description of street kids around a candy store
(pp. 560 ff.). However, the fervent sentimentality may not illustrate the avowals that New York City life is good because it is
"a society of sub-societies" (p. 553) and "had many of the
charms of a small town" but without the restrictions. Even village New York, of course, has its classic "dilemmas," as with the
psycho-fable of six-year-old St. Wayward fatally stabbing his
father Lothair (after he had taught that midget Prometheus how
to elaborately make a fire). The garbling of forms, in a melange
of realism and fairytale, didactic documentary and forced fantasy,
is mostly just confusing.

The final sections include other dallying with synthetic symbols and rituals, such as dancing as an answer to sexual decline in marriage (necessary after five years, following the gospel of Reich). Goodman's meandering anatomy also includes other ruminations, on such subjects as speeding as masturbation, potency compensation, self-destruction, and so on (pp. 467 ff.). There are more rhetorical appeals to Taoistic metaphors to answer the muddles of disturbed bohemians. Answers in this pastiche "educational romance" (p. 429) to the earlier-trumpeted "dilemma" also take the didactic form of a triple slogan announced at a coyly pompous town meeting of the Empire villagers: "Have another ounce of strength just to survive. . . . Go about your business to find what your business is. Be handy with some definite detail" (p. 591). Dr. Chuang-Reich-Goodman seems to be an uneducable Pangloss. This therapeutic chatter also includes such practical proposals as transforming playground periods "on the principles of character analysis and eurythmics" (p. 593). But lest we forget that the author is really a poet, an epilogue is provided Horatio—a mishmash of antique metaphors about carrying an "eloquent trumpet," some "arrows of desire," and "the mirror of Perseus" in order to defy an unappreciative world (pp. 620–21). So ends this multiple would-be novel. While it has many unintentional absurdities, its pretenses at humor inevitably succumb to obsessive vanity and anxiety. Any intellictual quality gets fractured by self-indulgent artiness. *The Empire City* may be a symptomatic hobby-horse, but the social criticism gets ridden better elsewhere. The work, at best, remains only a curiosity, the bumbling imperial conceit of a literary eccentric.[18]

II *Parental Firing*

Goodman also attempted a somewhat more conventional novel than the pastiche *Empire City*, a first-person account of a homosexual teacher that apparently drew heavily on his year's employment in a progressive boarding school (Manumit, 1943–44). *Parents' Day* (1951)[19] is a weak novel in its often portentously ruminative writing and in broad incompetence in continuing description. Crucial characters are not presented, such as the narrator's son who is living with him and is important to the parenting theme, and the women are quite unrealized.[20] Awkward flashbacks, sloppy narrative devices, and the insertion of stilted bits of verse further weaken the narrative. The book also shows an odd mixture of sexual bluntness and reticence, which can only partly be blamed on the censorship of the times. Disparities between avowals and presentation seem unintentional, as with the narrator's repeatedly telling the reader, "I was a good teacher" when his predatory sexuality, vanity, caprice, self-pity, and contempt for others (including the students he seduces) makes that quite doubtful.[21]

In half-confessional and somewhat murky fact, that disparity provides the theme which calls, in conveniently italicized but clotted declaration, for a changed character and community in which *"the innocence of immediate actions would be the general understanding"* (p. 160). In other words, seducing kids should not be understood as ill-motivated. This demand for homosexual acceptance turns about pained disparity between words and actions, "between my poetic self, the unafraid master of consistent speech, and my cowering self of immediate acts" (p. 161), though the issue complicates because of *two* voices, the "natural" and that of "my sick self." But his inconsistency between sexual avowals and actions is confusing. The narrator seems to be rejecting his wife, disguisedly; she visits the school (though she is only vaguely presented) and he concludes, "I didn't satisfy her sexually" (p. 49), though who is being rejected by her pregnancy by another man is unclear.[22] He is also having his child, and himself, mothered by a woman at the school—"unsatisfactory but not unpleasant sex" (p. 156)—which, however, depends on his casual affairs with soldiers from the nearby army base (undescribed) and intense affairs with several boys at the school. The women, then, may be unsatisfactory surrogates for male lovers. But another, and reverse, explanation (which I have also heard from several admitted bisexuals) suggests boys as sexual substitutes for girls. While watching adolescents, he muses, "When I was that very age, threats and punishments, and ineptitude and hurt pride, made me turn from the girls to the boys for easy love; and this habit persisted by attaching to itself some earlier desire that I no longer remember; and this desire persisted by

120   PAUL GOODMAN

warding off some still more forgotten terror" (p. 8). Reenforced
by equally vague anxieties of fear and rejection, the sexuality
becomes a guiltily compulsive pattern. Yet the pursuit of boys
is finally also a pursuit of women, he tells us: "Always it was not
these boys I was bent for, but in the end the mothers of these
boys" (p. 128). In terms of the action, that seems not very true,
though this thirtyish man several times rather ambiguously tries
and fails to relate to the older mother of his erotically favorite
seventeen-year-old. To get the mother, he notes, would be "the
source of well-being" and to recreate himself as his father, thus
"to unmake the damage in myself" (p. 128). The narrator several
times refers to his neurotic fear of rejection from his mother
(p. 140)—obviously Goodman's mother—and compulsively seeks
rejection while bitterly complaining of it (p. 165). The eroticism, then, doubles back on itself in several ways: boys in place
of girls, wives as surrogates for boys, boys as surrogates for their
mothers, mothers as girls to recreate himself as his father, and
all the sexual acting-out to make up for self-rejection by assert-
ing the imperious self. In such a pattern, "homosexuality" (no
doubt there are several different kinds) may be not so much a
"nature" or an "aberration," a propensity of its own or an en-
forced condition, as a labyrinthine dramatization of yearning
and rejection, and the guilty yearning for rejection which requires both ambiguous submission and violation. Some such
pattern, I suggest, may be found in Goodman's notorious bisexuality.

The double-bind of simultaneous humiliation and defiance,
which applies to the sexual action, leaves uncertain whether the
pursuit of the boys is cause or effect of the narrator's being rejected from the school community (p. 143). Homosexuality,
whether or not defensively, *may* be the cause of the narrator's
conspiring to have someone else replace the director of the
school, but Goodman's evasive handling leaves this far from
clear or candid. Earlier, the narrator noted, "I wished that I
were at last unmasked, my homosexual aims and intellectual
pretensions and acts of envy" (p. 76), so that he could be
accepted and loved in spite of the spiteful sexuality. Inevitably,
one of the boys confesses. The narrator admits "overt" sex to
the director and resigns, ending job and community. He appears

to have been expecting it, perhaps demanding it. The curious rationalization: "I knew it was not homosexuality but sexuality they were afraid of; but I did not know what in my own behavior was love and what was spite and the need to destroy excellence" (p. 205). The "excellence" I take to be the possibility of community that continuing at the school represents, and which this communitarian longs for but must simultaneously alienate himself from. This may also be the paradoxical basis of Goodman's politics generally.

More than defensively, perhaps, the narrator insists "that the children could not live [fully and freely] because their parents did not make them economically independent and our school did not grant them sexual autonomy" (p. 133). Identifying with the adolescents he wishes to seduce, he "resolved to battle according to common reason for the sexual opportunity of these dear young people . . ."(p. 77)—boys, of course. He does try to encourage the seventeen-year-old he lusts for to have sex with a fifteen-year-old girl, obtains condoms for him, and argues with the adults at the school for a place and acceptance of student sex. Admirably, Goodman here seems to be one of the first Americans to give public succor for adolescent sexuality, shocking in the 1940s. While some of the novelistic candor on homosexuality may derive from Gide, and the specific recommendations on adolescent sexuality from Reich's *The Sexual Revolution*, to make it part of progressive schooling seems peculiarly American. In one of the better lines in this often awkward novel, he poignantly notes of sexual repression that it is adding "more drops of poison, unacted out desire, to the misery of the world" (p. 103).

The other miseries which concern Goodman often relate to the lack of community (rather than justice or equality). The claimed appeal of the progressive school is as a free community which could provide an appropriate home for the bohemian artist; "we were the salt of the earth, the 'lunatic fringe,' with our schools as our communities" (p. 126).[23] Teaching as the succoring of artists as well as their use for community occasions provides the cultural laying on of hands—perhaps a bit literally! Goodman also suggests the process of intentional community: from the endless meetings arise new consenual values; from the fusion of the generations in common purpose comes the possibility of creating a larger than individual heritage—in a Goodmanian phrase, sensible ways of being in the world.[24] But a deeper purpose also shows through, the longing for a substitute family. Thus Goodman, who felt himself the abandoned child, concludes *Parents' Day* with some suggestive, though inadequately dramatized and developed, thoughts on parentage, really just on fatherhood, as carrying out "simple necessity" (p. 221) beyond the calculus of the ego.[25] To be a true parent is an end in itself. And he analogizes parenthood, I take it from the rather loose prose, to proper functioning of both culture and community. A true community would accept him, in his artistic as well as sexual peculiarity, which is his only way out of feeling "worthless and unwanted" (p. 223—"I am here speaking for all my artist friends" he unconvincingly adds).[26] Such an improbably indulgent community would restore paradisical innocence by caring for the invert (artist) as a father cares for a son—or should! This is poignant, though not as focused and probing as it should be, which is also how I would characterize this whole pedagogical would-be fiction.[27] One might note also that it is a bit better than the pretentious pastiche of *The Empire City*, though obscured by charred motives and writing.

III *Making Done as a Novelist*

Paul Goodman's final novel, *Making Do* (apparently written in the fall of 1962), continues many of the peculiar concerns of his earlier novels, though inevitably with some change of tone by a man in his fifties. "I draw the older man . . . quite literally from myself" (he confesses in *Little Prayers*, p. 27). Again the subject is the life of urban marginals; a major theme is the longing for community; a majority of the figures are male adolescents (with perhaps an increased proportion of psychopaths); and we can see the usual authorial eccentricities, conceits, and self-pity. The closest of his works to the realistic conventions, documentation somewhat reduces stilted writing. Though irregular, the presentation of the "street people"—college dropouts and Puerto Rican hustlers—shows some verisimilitude with their dissociated responses and fractured ritualism. He recognizes "how empty and desperate the street life" (p. 128) is as the young (and not so young) descend into gratuitous violence, schizophrenic break-downs, stupid pregnancies (though Goodman weirdly seems to approve of this), crime and prison, catatonic withdrawal, or desperate conventionality. *Making Do* may be granted some sad documentary utility.

But the larger reach remains problematic, the yoking of this nightmarish marginal disintegration with the national lunacies. The loosely presented radical actions—a Ban the Bomb demonstration, with its police riot; the picketing against meaningless voting; the off-key personal messiahism of Goodman's social and political theorizing—seem to lack necessary connection with the marginal and delinquent: "It takes a lot of bad education, a venal economy, and a really insane foreign policy to achieve that hoodlum strut, that junkie slouch, that hipster cool . . ." (p. 231). Perhaps the problem is that the real hoodlums and hipsters of our national junk and international jive reside elsewhere than the pathetic street scenes. Nor does substantiation come from a bit of thinly crude satire of an upper-middle class suburban family in Mount Kisco who are shrilly accused but not shown in high delinquency—"they and their class were destroying the country, its youth, and Western civilization" (p. 257). Probably misfocused, it is also, as put, just foolish spite against the upper-suburbanites Goodman always despised.[28]

In the making of *Making Do*, Goodman did not adequately fuse its rhetoric of indignation and its novelistic techniques. Related disproportions appear with the coy narrator, the "tired friend," "the weary one," "the old man," "the communitarian anarchist," the conference-hopping, moralistic, smug pop-sociologist—patently Paul Goodman, though someone else is coyly so named—and his homosexual affair with a twenty-year-old college drop-out and disciple, Terry. While some of the irregular detailing of this central relationship seems promising—the adolescent's hostile-submissive manner, his "self-centeredness" which was "insufferably boring" (p. 71) to the self-centered narrator, and his descent into schizophrenia—little novelistic evidence appears for Terry's asserted "genius" in communalism (p. 211), his supposed intellectual "brilliance," or his counter-culture role-playing (blamed on the influence of Mailer). Also, a most odd reticence covers his sexual and other dependence on his ideologue "master." The narrator's relation with the adolescent gets partly rationalized on pedagogical and compassionate grounds, but even on the terms given (p. 81) is exploitative, as, I suppose, continuing sexual demands on any object of contempt must be. This sickly ambivalence applies broad scale, as with the hostile-abject relations of the other adults in the book to the adolescent hustlers. Raising it to a level of classical ponderousness, as when the narrator explains to his "young disciple" that his admiration of the successful is "the argument of Thrasymachus in Plato's *Republic*" (p. 144), which of course suggests the narrator as Socrates, rather more reveals than disguises the falsity and grossness.

The issue goes beyond sexual acting-out to the whole perspective of the book since role-playing crudely dominates the narrator as well as the lesser hustlers.[29] A patently bad teacher, he uncritically sees himself, and most of the other pop-intellectual *lüftmenschen,* as doing a fine job at the lectures and forums and conferences on urban problems—electrifying the students (p. 31), his own statements leaving them "buzzing with pride" (p. 43), and his own gestures as "fantastic" (p. 39). Equally modest about his other poses, he claims but doesn't show that he is the "champion" (p. 44) of adolescents, taking on the knightly heroism and "thankless task" out of pure "citizenly" concern, no doubt lustily. By his very lack of specific vocation and involvement (after all, he was really an "artist"), he can grandiloquently claim, "I had a job with the youth of America . . ." (p. 73), without taking much continuing responsibility, unlike a teacher or social worker. Essentially, Goodman engaged in the pretentious role-playing of which he accused Mailer and other exploiters of professionalized egotism.

"Youth" provided his vice and his game, which he turned into a well-applauded and well-paid "profession," though with such earnestness that he may have done some good. He does offer some apologetics for the public racketeering of pop-sociologist, at which, probably, his eccentric ways provided some enlivening oddity. The "kind of Americans who did ask my opinion were uniformly benevolent, good-humored, confused. By paying me well, according to their absurdly inflated standard, they legitimatized opposition, as they ruthlessly went their way" (p. 100). Yet he also likes to think of his coopted role-playing of youth-champion as the result of his prudent persistence and intellectual talent (p. 101). But his smug treatment of himself and the other performers who provided "earnest thought with existential vitality" (p. 203)—little evident in the novel[30]—shows a self-serving crassness which denies the most pertinent intellectual talent, honesty.

Dishonesty inclines one to mawkishness, and there is considerable of that in *Making Do*. Some comes out as self-pity: "I was now fifty-three years old, and I could count on very few happy hours that I had had" (p. 212)—he must be excluding the thousands of hours speechifying to and copulating with a multitude of boys and girls. Some comes out as stock tear-jerker, such as the extended mourning for his cocker spaniel accidentally killed by a car (pp. 87 ff.). The usual other side of the sentimental is the resentful, and there is some of that in the narrator's condemnation of his shadowily presented wife for being jealous of his sex with girls and boys, and for being "boring" and "disloyal" about his role-playing (p. 155). Maudlin-nasty bits appear about other figures, too. But then, as Goodman later explained in an interview, it was "a novel about people not making the scene . . ."; in *Making Do* they're all fuck-ups."[31] Surely the narrating author is.

All end vaguely sad, with many of the lesser hustlers jailed on drug, violence and sex charges. But then we get allegory! A quite undeveloped character, Amos, an errant and threatening husband of one of the marginal women, has returned from Israel quieted down and ready to start over—"Making his own choices" (p. 276). I suppose this points to the acceptance indicated by the title. The narrator also makes do with his unhappiness since he thinks he has produced some valuable ideas. The summation idea is that he has recreated the Platonic "ladder of love" by going from love of bodies to love of virtuous character to love of his world—"a man's eros turns to the institutions and customs of the city" (p. 274). Still, he has a way to go since "frozen on the ladder, I did not feel any peace of God." The reader may be tempted to tell him that for the ladder, as for this rickety scaffold of a novel, he is the wrong man in the wrong place. But perhaps the epilogue quote—John Robinson to the Pilgrims embarking for America: "The Lord has yet more light and truth to break forth" (p. 276)—claims some sort of divine access to replace the lack of human access. While there are some suggestive social (and symptomatic) bits, this rough document of sexual and sociological hustling can hardly make do as an even passable novel. Perhaps fortunately, then, Paul Goodman's next decade of prolific writing took to other modes which gave a nonegotistical subject a chance, instead of obviously inappropriate literary fiction.[32]

IV Unstorying

Paul Goodman published sixty or so pieces he apparently thought of as stories—the uncertainty here is because of want of a definition for writings that consist of a melange of sketches, essays, exercises, fragments, notes, and hardly readable poetical stuffing. Through persistence and friends, he managed to publish many in "little magazines" and then collected them in four volumes (about twenty remained unpublished). His incomplete collected stories, *Adam and His Works* (1968), contains forty-one items (while appearing to range over thirty-five years, only the poorly written title piece seems to have been produced in the last decade).[33] His pretense at writing stories for so long seems puzzling since he mostly wrote badly, and after much practice wrote worse. The pieces show almost no ability at continuing narrative or dramatization or character development or pointed description. While the ostensible modes vary—realism, fantasy, allegory, joke, myth, abstract fable, personal memoir, didactic anecdote—most of the works grossly violate their own conventions and many just disintegrate into ponderous or coy ruminations. Few do not have painful violations of subject and point of view and tone and style—especially authorial intrusions. The predominant form might be called ruminative pastiche, with schizoid tendencies.

Apparently sensing that something was peculiar about his stories (and plays), by the 1940s Goodman rationalized his manner as literary "cubism" to justify an uncontrollable wandering from subject and theme into reflexive abstractions.[34] This further allowed the sketches to avoid most simple coherence and readable graces of concrete description of person and place.[35] But even the ruminative metaphors and generalizations don't come off well because of incompetent writing: trite, flowery, pedantic, cute, pretentious, disconnected, muddled, and endlessly awkward. They mostly monument conceited peculiarity and self-indulgence.

Rather than belabor the obvious with tiresome examples, let me briefly comment on what are probably the four best pieces of the forty-one in the collected "stories" (the twenty or so posthumously published pieces belong with the poorer ones). Most consistent and developed of the early stories is a reflective sketch about some problems in writing a fiction, "The Detective Story" (1935). The inability to write a detective story leads the writer to pursue further information, the practice of crime, the problems of logic, the philosophy of morals, each supposedly deepening the issue of detecting endless ambiguity. The obviously imitation-Kafka conclusion:

Now it may be granted that I, too, shall one day be shown where and what I ought properly to work at, and what is to be the end of it. But I know, and this is the fourth maxim I have discovered, that by myself I shall never be able to find this out. For first I learned that to understand the motives of the criminal one must first put oneself in his place; and then I saw that before that I had to learn the truth about myself, for who but myself was I to put in the place of the criminal; but thirdly I came to see that before anything one must have some criterion of the truth itself (and even if I had it how would I know that it was a true one?). But now I understand, or hope I do, that whereas from my side I cannot go on with this work, I need not despair but only wait, or need only despair and wait.[36]

Perhaps a takeoff on Kafka's "Don't despair, not even that you don't despair," and on the inept author's persisting sense of having no vocation or place in the world, the conception is defensively arch. While the prior detailing is rather too abstract and the sense of the world callow, this unusually clean writing and logical development show some literary discipline to compensate for a lack of natural responsiveness and talent. Few of his other pieces do.

A story of a few years later that got some attention, "The Facts of Life" (1940),[37] is a period-piece brittle satire of an urban upper-middle class secularized Jewish family of the time and sort that makes "adjustments belonging to Jews of a certain class of money" (*Adam*, p. 49) when confronting mild anti-Semitism. In somewhat plausible though forced dialogue and fashionably identifiable scenes (such as the Museum of Modern Art), it unfolds around the nine-year-old daughter in a private school who wants to know why she has been insultingly called a "juice." She knows nothing about Jewish identification. Defensively, her father simultaneously denies that there is such a thing as Jewishness and asserts that Jews disproportionately produce genius. The anxious upwardly mobile wife concludes that if "it weren't for the Jews there wouldn't be anti-Semitism" (*Adam*, p. 59). The points and characters show some verisimilitude, though there are intrusive shifts, including dubious authorial sociologizing about the violence of anti-Semitic gentile boys and the imposition on the little girl of one of Freud's sillier notions, the female "castration complex," which is to be taken as another of the puzzling ambiguous facts of life. The ambivalence about Jewish identity, expressed as well as satirized, appears elsewhere in Goodman, a secularized urban Jew (uncertain middle class but raised poor) in an insistently Jewish peer-culture which he seems to have both exalted and resented.[38] Most odd for Goodman is not the ethos but the relatively realistic discipline of the story, so contrary to most of his other writing, and so variant in style as to be a striking fluke. In fact, no later fiction of Goodman's reaches the even minor level of story competence of "The Facts of Life."

But a later travel essay, published and republished as a story, does show some passable detailing, "Our Visit to Niagara."[39] The unpleasantness of the undisguised author centers the story and provides the ironic point. He says "for though I have come to lead among people a spiteful and miserable existence, I am still simple enough to be entranced by a geological splendour" (*Adam*, p. 360). Except that he isn't. The spiteful antagonism of the narrator to his wife, a dim figure with a sentimental feeling for Niagara from childhood experience, leads to sometimes shrewdly edgy details about the falls as a nonexperience because of its commercial carricaturing into an "American Hoax" (*Adam*, p. 367). Resenting that his wife won't be more submissive to his demands and contempt, the narrator "bravely enough" scorns her and the geological splendour but smugly makes use of both to "hammer out my impressions of Niagara Falls" (*Adam*, p. 370). While anxious conceit blocks the piece from developing the humor, it does provide a satiric sense (intentional or not) of a pompously resentful writer as American tourist, which has some genuineness.

A number of other pieces published as stories are also travel sketches and exposés of petulant egotism. The best of them, and probably the best piece in the collected stories, is "A Statue of Goldsmith," which records part of Goodman's 1957 touring of Ireland.[40] A wry personal emphasis: "For I contrive, often with ingenuity and boldly seizing opportunities, to get in a situation where I can be alone and do as I please, and then I am lonely and 'doing what I please' does not get me what I want" (p. 412). So with his literary efforts; he feels positive about having completed an important project (probably *The Empire City*, which ends with some Irish folderol) but dissatisfied. After unsuccessful homosexual advances to a young workingman ("instinctively chary of me"), he wanders around Trinity University library and ruminates on the statue of Oliver Goldsmith. At first he feels smugly at home because "my doctorate was a sound one" and "I securely belonged to the inner company of these authors, scholars, and doctors." Pathetic, but further reflection on the statue undercuts the pomposity by raising questions as to why it was there: Out of love for Goldsmith? Or guilt about not having loved him enough during his life? Or for the society's own aggrandizement? He concludes that the honoring of Goldsmith has little to do with the man or his work, or anyone's living relation to either, but is part of cultural abstraction. His smugness as learned author fantasizing his immortality is superceded by a sense of futility, even "horror": "And I thought of us ghouls in the University close, who passed on our culture, just for the immortality of it. Like a clench of the fist. Like the statue of Goldsmith" (p. 418). Such displaced and mortuary motives, as with his own earlier smug

self-regard for his literary work, deny animal spirits and the
immediate and lively human.

Goodman's writing rarely achieves this degree of presented
insight (intentional or not). Here instead of cultural pretensions he has had the interesting honesty for once to admit, "I
am very inept" (p. 415), and to go with it. But it is gross
ineptness in other senses which dominates the stories. By pick-
ing the four best I may be giving a falsely positive impression;
after all, one is a nonstory by definition, one is patently a fluke,
and two are uncharacteristically self-satirizing personal travel
essays.

No doubt Goodman would have thought more representative
of his work the six ragged and poorly written callow sketches
of *The Break-Up of Our Camp* (originally written in the mid-
1930s and revised in 1942 and 1947) about his last year as a
counselor in a Zionist youth camp. They contain heavily allegorical bits about a strange canoeist, the problem of obtaining
ten Jews for a *minyan* (and some authorial ambivalence about
Jewishness, with perhaps the muddled closing down of the camp
a comment on the ethnic heritage), and poorly described hitch-
hiking. The writing is heavy—"I was in the presence of what I
should do well to disregard not lightly" (*Adam*, p. 217). The
homosexuality is arch: "But it was, is, too late to fall in love
with the boy, myself, just because my world has fallen into
chaos. Longing for immortality" (*Adam*, p. 225). The one amusingly stilted rumination: "I had of course the one function that
I ever committed myself to, to have a hard-on in impractical
circumstances" (*Adam*, p. 228).

Or perhaps Goodman would have selected "The Galley to
Mytilene," a heavy-handed allegory about being compassionate
to enemies, with a pedantic use of Greek mythology, or "A
Statue of Nestor" with its murkily portentous play with Homeric
materials, or "The Death of Aesculapius," which I take to be
using its creaking Greek machinery for self-analysis and self-
pity about a doctor who could not cure himself. Or since Goodman thought highly of the poorer sort of Hawthorne, he might
have picked "Iddings Clark," a picture of a schoolteacher going
to pieces, for no particular reason, who "saw on each face a
veil. It was the black veil in the harrowing story of Hawthorne,

from which I have taken the motto for this story" (*Adam,* p. 128). The teacher ends up naked in class and is led away. Or perhaps "Jeremy Owen," a totally implausible mix of reportage and parable about a small-town "border-line-insane" youth who gets excited about space shots—the only other who does is a "youth of lofty aspiration" who "wouldn't dast to cry in public"— and leaves town, to end in New York's Museum of Modern Art, where a character named Paul Goodman explains Monet to him, has a conversation with "Everyman," and concludes that it's a lousy country with its lack of space-patriotism but we must "Foster Excellence!" (*Adam,* pp. 3–26). Or perhaps it would be "The Old Knight," a meandering and inconsistent fairy tale about a Knight with an "artist heart": "I myself, I wore out my heart reaching for the community that was in fact amongst us; and for it I got nothing but abuse as an irresponsible utopian." But eventually the noble one gets "invitations to lecture at the university to 'stir things up,' because the youth were becoming too comformist!" (*Adam,* pp. 102–108) His opponents, of course, are "a cult of knights demented" who favor alienation or are sexually repressed or teach at universities to get grants or—the one suggestive point—think life is complicated instead of just hard.

But enough. The personal pomposities, and the taste for the fabulistic but without the discipline, say, of a Malamud, produce a stilted flatulence. In no serious way can Goodman be considered even a very minor short story writer. Why, in a nearly forty year writing career, didn't he recognize the obvious incompetence and badness of his fictional attempts? Of course there is that horrendous and self-indulgent egotism and the entrapping self-identification as literary "artist." Yet, I suggest, not only the ironies of several of the better sketches but other things show that, in some sense, he did know. The repeated and awkward switching of modes, the crass intrusions into and violations of so many sketches, the refusal (for a genre critic yet!) to distinguish notes, essays, allegories, fantasies, documents, from each other, and the indifference to even minimal competence—these suggest a deep implicit self-attack in the writings on the adolescent role-playing of story writer. As soon as Goodman found a more successful writing role, as middle-aged social

critic and libertarian gadfly, he pretty much gave up writing
stories, as if in confirmation that it had mostly been a mistaken
vocation. Only hobbyist touches continued. It often has taken
American males a long time to grow up.

V *Playing Around*

Why Goodman published eighteen attempts at plays is not
altogether clear. Since he had little sense of dramatization, character, effective dialogue, formal order, consistent language, or
any sort of theatrical style, or even interesting stage business,
drama would seem embarrassingly inappropriate. But Goodman's embarrassment threshold was exceptionally high. He had
no aesthetic super-ego. Most of the productions of his plays
known to me were by his political associates and friends, such
as Julian Beck and Judith Malina of the Living Theatre, and
appear to have been badly received.[41] However, Goodman's
theatre interest arose early; a friend got him a job for three
summers as a counsellor putting on plays with children. He
also did some traditional graduate work in literature which, of
course, included classical drama, and he used examples of it
in his doctoral dissertation. He also apparently helped put on
one or more plays at a progressive school where he taught.[42]
These experiences may have misled him. He also lived the larger
part of his life in New York City, where theater receives a perhaps exaggerated attention though drama has been mostly a
minor and poor American literary form, in comparison with
novels, movies, personal poetry, memoirs, poetic-prose docu-
mentaries, and several other genres. But plays do appear to be
a communal art, and the notion of servicing a community always
appealed to Goodman. Indeed, he suggested the lack of real
community as cause of his artistic limitation; he wrote, he noted,
"in isolation . . . in conditions that do not allow fraternal conflict, out of which comes what one did not know one knew."[43]
Because, as a marginal figure, he did not write for a community,
or for entertainment, or for other professional or practical purpose, his poor literary efforts in damatic form might best be
viewed as a not very playful playing around.

Some relatively early writing includes five playlets published as *Stop-Light* (1941). This late-juvenilia loosely connects with Japanese Noh drama, he explains, in its ritualization of "states of awareness." The pedantry here is unironic and precious imitation of bits of impersonal form for slight personal moments. "Dusk" has vague figures and a chorus, some tritely archaic images (moon and gold), muddled syntax and reiterations, around an inchoate sense of family loss in New Jersey. "The Birthday" has figures named "Paul" and "Birthday," flat quotations from Virgil and Dante, and some vague melancholy around a young man's skittish sense of aging. Clichés dominante ("voices hoarse as foghorns"), and some are ridiculously muddled: "Laughing pierced my heart" (he means laughter?) and "moonlit face is pink" (a visual impossibility). The most developed playlet, entitled "The 3 Disciplines," has, besides the usual chorus, a "Poet" and a "Demon of Boundaries." It ruminates ponderously about poetic discipline, foolishly claiming chess, music and mathematics, which are vulgarly identified as especially Jewish, as the prototypes. Poet Paul admits a conflict between his poetical impulses and discipline, concluding, "Alas for me! I cannot write a word,/hemmed on all sides by modesty and doubt." But he escapes this good sense because "Life, the great dragon" is quite beyond discipline. So is "The Cyclist" in which a figure identified as "Poem" summarizes the Platonist doctrine of "eternal forms"—by "love and abstraction are they known, a process of 2 steps." In fact, the process seems to be a "vivid memory" of a biking trip fancied to amorphousness ("my mind is wandering far as in a dream"). "The Stop-Light" is a traffic signal on a deserted road with the poet as a fearful driver. He sees an old wreck which gives him a pang of mortality, made poetical by repeating three times "the moments fly by like a snowstorm/and my time is slipping away."[44] I suppose he means snowflakes, and for the reader to slip into his self-pathos.

But he didn't slip into any better writing when he turned to would-be comedy in 1941 with *Jonah*,[45] a tedious, flat pastiche retelling of the Old Testament story and some bad Yiddish jokes by "a fat little Jew." The bad jargon (finalize, feedback, and so on) and the period euphemisms (frig) were not revised out in the reprinting many years later. The reductive conception of Jonah as *goycup*-dumb does not help the earnest theme of New

York as Nineveh, a city supposedly saved by the deity's forgiveness but, in Goodman's treatment, apparently because its king was also a dummy.

The turn, a few years later, to would-be imitation neoclassical melodrama, *Faustina* (1948)[46] is no improvement. A pedantically sententious Marcus Aurelius acts out the covertly "sadistic homosexual" and jealous tyrant to his raunchy-hysterical wife. The characterization lacks consistency and the form is crudely mechanical (though there is a daring possibility at the end for the actress, we are told, to step out of character). Goodman's usual language difficulties here grossly muddle archaicism (a-mouldering, yonder, nay elixir, intellective, hither, lust, lewd, hath) with American colloquialisms (screw, cunt, score, dig, hiya, four-bit, lots of shit, guts, hot in the pants), though the drama is supposedly high in scene and style.

The Young Disciple (1954) was produced in the mid-1950s by Goodman's friends in the Living Theatre. Appropriate to their performing style are indications of much nonverbal stage business. But these could hardly carry the portentously arch vagaries of dialogue about a loosely Christ-like "Our Master." The learned purpose here seems to be to demonstrate quasi-religious responses of misunderstanding and persecution, though without any substantial material or vision, which results in loose theatrical pedantry. Apparently the unappreciated messiah-figure is Paul Goodman since he has snatches of his typical rhetoric and habits. Some results in farce—"OUR MASTER dances his dance of Fucking the Only World." In a note to the play, Goodman says the material comes out of Buber, his own psychoanalyzing of the Gospels, and his therapeutic doctrine of emphasizing "the pre-verbal elements of theatre: outcries and gasping, bawling and giggling, trembling, breathing hard, throwing tantrums and throwing punches." More likely, the stage business comes, in reductive fashion, from Artaud.[47] Goodman also tells us that his lack of theatrical success results from the incompetence of the actors and of the audience, which prefers to be manipulated, rather than from his own psychopathic but undramatic self-pity.[48]

Goodman also puttered for some years with a series of linked playlets entitled *The Family of Abraham*, performed by the

Living Theatre in 1959, reportedly first sketched out in 1935. Three of the pieces were published (at least one more remains unpublished), over the years, in periodicals. *Abraham and Isaac* is a sometimes poetical account (that is, it has partial rhyme and some inverted syntax) of the preparations for the Old Testament scene of sacrifice. We find the author's usual mixture of slang, cliche, pomposity and flat repetitions, though God thees-and-thous inconsistently. In "Notes on Abraham"[49] Goodman pretentiously attacks existentialist interpretations (probably with Kierkegaard's *Fear and Trembling* in mind) for a simpler view. In this play he almost totally deintellectualizes the would-be sacrifice, supposedly to show simple faith in the nature of things, but only succeeds in making the whole absurdly trivial. *Hagar and Ishmael* continues the awkward writing and stilted action with a confusedly defiant Ishmael arguing with an angel. Goodman's note tells us that Ishmael was to become "the father of the Arabians." *The Cave at Machpelah* has him meeting with Isaac to bury Abraham. With supposedly contemporary relevance (1958), the top Jew and the top Arab reconcile at lunch. Goodman means it to be emphatically affirmative stuff; the stage directions for a character crying "My-Lord!" to an angel read: "a totally given affirmation: to be, somehow, the climax of all these plays about Abraham." We also know that it reaches positive thinking because the same exact speech about "how goodly" things are gets repeated five times.

Like the hobbyist who indiscriminately stores in his garage any old hubcaps or old blue glass, Goodman stored in publications any old pseudoliterary gestures. These might be funny in their unintentional burlesque, in their lack of even minimal taste and writing competence, if they were not so earnestly pretentious, and therefore so pathetic. This also applies to his last collection of drama, *Tragedy & Comedy, Four Cubist Plays* (published in 1970 but perhaps revisions of things roughed out earlier when he had pretensions to literary imitations of cubism). They are crude pedantic exercises. "Structure of Tragedy, *after Aeschylus*" should be taken as early Greek because of the machinery of masks, chorus and totemism (following Cambridge anthropology). It should also be taken as the usual Goodmanian verbal muddle of jargon (communicable), archaicisms (marrow,

curst, empyrean), slang (hard-on), and triteness. It has one
redeeming though contextless line (probably a direct quote from
a conversation with the eccentric historian Benjamin N. Nelson):
"The use of history is to keep alive old defeated causes."[50]

"Structure of Tragedy, *after Sophocles*" is another self-de-
feated quasi-classical cause, a fragment essentially empty in
content, inverted in syntax, muddled in diction, ostensibly
Sophoclean in awkward motifs of self-division and fate (mis-
understood as "luck"). "Structure of Pathos, *after Euripides*"
shows that Goodman read *The Trojan Women* and *The Bacchae*
in the arbitrary Chicago-school manner, that he confused "frightful" with frightened, and that he, too, can put a god on stage.
The later concludes for his "frightful" woman-hating author:
"I don't like this information/about Women's Liberation:/
Mother Earth is a psychopath," ending fearsomely "and the Ice
Age comes again." A different sort of bigotry informs "Little
Hero, *after Moliere*," which is supposedly comic in its use of
mistaken identity, a made-up, leaden-ear, antique mode of street
jive, and the victory of a pathetic-tough bright kid over all the
regular guys. I suppose the kid is also Paul Goodman—there is
not much of anyone else in his unimaginative writings—a kid
who never got over his adolescent traumas and never grew up
into a dramatist, though he kept playing around with his literary
hobby.

VI   *Poetasting*

Paul Goodman was not much of a poet though he wrote verse
off and on most of his adult life, but perhaps more in his later
years when he had given up pretensions to drama and fiction.
He was working on his *Collected Poems* in the weeks before his
death at sixty.[51] With his usual unselfcritical persistence, he
had managed not only to publish much of his verse but to view
his identity as "Poet." Perhaps that was part of the difficulty for
he played antique stock-poet—thee'd and thou'd, awkwardly
inverted syntax, splattered around flowery clichés, and often
belabored traditional forms (the ballad, the sonnet, the ballade,
and various classical imitations which come out as parodies).[52]
When in some late verses he wrote "in Victorian stanzas . . . I

will praise the nature of things" (*CP*, p. 227), he partly identified but did not understand his poetic problem of imposing tired
formal order on his most peculiar sensibility.[53]

Given his avowed poetic of "common reason," curative natu-
ralness, colloquial speech and "plain facts"—writing them literally down/is all the poetry I can" (*CP*, p. 68)—one might have
expected him to struggle towards something on the order of
William Carlos Williams's open forms, simple line-phrasing
based on colloquial speech, and the immediacy of the object.[54]
But instead of going with or beyond modernism in American
poetry, this social revolutionary mostly missed "the revolution
of the word" in an eccentric poetic pedanticism—really an open-
fly archaicism. It would have taken a master stylist—or at least
someone as clever as Empson or Ransom—to have made much
out of worn and residual poetic manners. But Goodman's problems with language, with obsessive self-conceit (and insularity
against criticism), and with not having appropriate forms for
his urban and peculiar experience, led to desperately searching
for poetical roles to play. He tried a variety of modes, from haiku
to synthetic dialect anecdotes. But most of it ends in mere
mannerism.[55]

A series of late verses, "Little Prayers," of which he seems to
have thought inordinately well, shows the unfortunate choice
he often made. These ninety-two plaints,[56] mostly eight-line,
are supposedly modest, though he speaks of his "genius," of
being "the conscience of my country" (p. 85), and of being
such a fine poet that "my voice/will afterwards be much ad-
mired/by the English scholars, Lord" (p. 94). But the difficulty
seems larger than a dubious conceit inappropriate to the prayer
form. By taking over the language and some of the manners of
stock prayers, we get a thick religiosity: dost, hast, whence,
thou, thy, deliverest, sin, Savior, God the Father, devil, paradise,
Holy Ghost, spiritual shipwreck, angel, Lord, eke out, lo!,
heavenly trumpets, elects to call, kingdom, moral armor, saved,
laden, garlands, shining ships, purgatory, angel, Master, blessed,
etc. We also get awkwardly twisted syntax to force rimes and
fit forms, such as "if today I throw/beaten my armor down"
(p. 77), "was God to Abraham did say" (p. 91), and "Now thou
Creator Spirit/him do not desert" (p. 78). This results in pieties

that seem to belong more to the metaphors and manners than to Paul Goodman—Jewish agnostic anarchist devoted to the Tao—such as "apprentice I wait His command" and "prayer to the Savior." I suppose, too, the placebo sentiments then become inevitable, such as "my hurts/are measured to my just deserts" (p. 79), "weariness and grief is a fair description of my life" (p. 87), "Rest well thy weary head and heart" (p. 78), and "for ever our task is measured to our power" (p. 74). No doubt Goodman did have some conservative, pious, masochistic attitudes, but, from the fuller perspective of his other writings, not in this heavy degree and sticky tone. The stock language and machinery of "prayers" in the pietistic Christian tradition seems to have taken over and, in spite of some forced qualifications ("God" is sometimes "common reason" and other connotations which violate sensible usage), the submissive religiosity tends to dominate in these mostly poor little plaints.[57] This might be called the fallacy of inexpressive form.[58]

Perhaps Goodman's inadequate poetic expression can be summarized in terms of one image, a favorite of his (*CP*, pp. 343, 365, 406, 426, and so on, and also in the prose), used to entitle a poem and a collection, and apparently a heartfelt epithet affirming the New Yorker's provincial loyalty to "The Lordly Hudson." In the poem of that name, the river (as elsewhere) doesn't get much tangible description: the misplaced designation of it as a "stream," the puzzling claim that it is "hardly flowing," the left-handed praise that it "has no peer in Europe or the East" (inadvertently bringing to mind that it is out-classed in the West), and mention of the "green-grown cliffs." I don't question the sincerity of Goodman's feeling for the "glory" of the Hudson River, or his personal identification with it as a sign of "home! home!", or even the improbable attribution of the epithet to (apparently) a bus driver or cabby, but repeating "Lordly" six times in a short poem is at best an awkwardly weak archaism without context and of dubious appropriateness. "Lordly Hudson" points less to a place or experience than to the eccentric mannerism of the versifier.[59]

This applies to many of Goodman's verses. In glancing at some other bits (for but few, to be noted, shape up to poems), we might keep in mind that incongruity seems to be his real poetic. Taken thus, the obsessive personal bathos—even he acknowledges once: "blind I am with brimming of self-pity" (*CP*, p. 375)—and the gross self-flattery serve as poetical adumbrations of oddity, and perhaps therefore must read oddly. Certainly the conceit is emphatic, as with his repeatedly announcing that America will put up a "statue in the park" to him (*CP*, pp. 17, 107, and in the prose), and "tourists come to see the very spot/like the relic in the crypt/ where he wrote" (*CP*, p. 46).[60] After all, as he several ways tells us, "I have well deserved of the Republic (*CP*, p. 187), as well as of many friends (*CP*, p. 436). This was not just because he stood "wiser than Socrates" (*CP*, p. 106), but because he was a "most excellent poet" (*CP*, p. 393, where a Christmas tree told him so), and because "I have among the Americans/the gift of honest speech" (*CP*, p. 290, in justification after treating his wife spitefully). For he has been the writer "to whom is given to declare . . . just how a thing is" (*CP*, p. 308; another version, p. 354), though the announcements rather edge out the practice. But who dare complain since "excellent sentences I make/better than any other man" (*CP*, p. 323). After all, God smiles upon Goodman as he writes (*CP*, p. 347); "shall I ungratefully/my gift of formal speech disdain?" (*CP*, p. 311). Not when he is one of our nobles: "New Yorker/talented Jew, I am by birth the royal family," and thus full of "*noblesse oblige*/magnanimous and paternalistic" (*CP*, p. 238). And he is also encouraged by God and "prophet-birds" to provide "the useful thoughts you have/for the Americans" (*CP*, p. 339). Incidentally, by "Americans" Goodman seems to mean other than his fellow New Yorkers, with their special mission of enlightenment; in some slight verses titled "New York" he notes "we have unhappy faces," but adds parenthetically "though human compared with the Americans" (*CP*, p. 429), which would seem to be the rest of the country. But even they deserve help, at least when "the Angel Fame" (*CP*, p. 305) is watching him or when he was "sketching a little book important for the nation" (*CP*, p. 124). While in various verses Goodman grants that his character was "bad," his "behavior was beneath contempt" (*CP*, p. 112), and he had a "blighted life" (*CP*, p. 194), yet his work would leave him "blameless because I did well" (*CP*, p. 69).

There is more of this candor of megalomania, which seems to be without intentional irony. It does provide relief of a sort from the complaining (not enough sex, appreciation, love, reputation, response, admiration, good reviews, beauty, domestic devotion, opportunity, health, luck and so on). The monstrous self-conceit may also help confirm his argument that "artists" make "a kind of psychopathic adjustment" (*CP*, p. 330).

Part of Goodman's adjustment to a desperate sense of need, lacking the usual super-ego limitations, was by the compulsive pursuit of sexual love, or as he labels it, "lust." In the verses, a few bits are heterosexual, though mostly out of duty—his wife in several poems, such as "fucking Sally to give her a baby" (*CP*, p. 110), which was his usual view of what women need— or out of *noblesse*—"but serviceably just because I can/I'll fuck her good and make one creature glad" (*CP*, p. 113), he says of a woman of whom he was contemptuous.[61] But most of his "lust" went toward boys, "young ass" (*CP*, p. 297). The situation often seems to have been what is called "cruising" (or sometimes identified by the pop-song euphemism of "Careless Love"—"I hunting cock, that's an unlicensed sport" [*CP*, p. 125], with an apparent but not exclusive emphasis on providing fellatio). He repeatedly complains, such as "God damn! a hundred people on a train, not one worth groping" (*CP*, p. 123). But the pursuit also included longer, and rather paternalistic, affairs with young men. Unfortunately, many of these accounts fail to be of much poetic interest because of descriptive inadequacies, as with a vague "David" (*CP*, pp. 217, 226, 231, 232; for an even more obscurely skittish example, see p. 421). Perhaps he lacked the machinery for a male Chloe; certainly he lacked a Genet's sense of detail.

Not only "queer" (*CP*, p. 228) but with some extreme proclivities, which Goodman attributes to his "lonesome life" and "sex-starved youth" (*CP*, p. 148), he feels trapped in the need for human responses in exploitative situations, often with homosexual prostitutes—a mouthful of words as well as other matter. He needs intellectual stimuli, for as a boy sexy things alone didn't arouse him, but "if I heard the causes of these things/my penis rose inquiring for more" (*CP*, p. 105); even as an old man, "when the interior sun of reason arises . . . red my penis spring alive" (*CP*, p. 396).[62] Flattered when his punks admire him as their "old artist and champion" (*CP*, p. 303), he is, however, irritated that most of them are not up to intellectual conversation, or at least to listening to it—"to me it is panic to be speechless" (*CP*, p. 278). "I am able to love only the kid/that I can talk to seriously" (*CP*, p. 219), but of course that violates the essential relation to a hustler.[63] Probably his best poem on this obsessive problem is a documentary-styled dialogue, "A Hustler" (*CP*, p. 292), in which he for once dramatizes what he usually just complains about. Or as he elsewhere puts his dilemma: "I felt contempt and my cock fell," for "if he didn't talk I was exasperated / and if he did talk I got angry" (*CP*, p. 230).

The other side of the pathetic desperation even appears several times, as in the brief reflection of a responsive lover-boy who compared Goodman's lusting to "insistent mosquitoes," though Goodman again excuses himself because of his "bleak childhood, unsure, abandoned, hungry" (*CP*, p. 126). And there is also the sad hypocrisy: "I say that 'I love you' more than I do—not lying,/it's an hypothesis I hope will be surprisingly confirmed" (*CP*, p. 224). And then there is the half-recognized bathos of "two grown men" who are "kissing and kissing" in the yearning of "two babes lost in the wood" (*CP*, p. 231). And then there is the rationalization for seducing the lads by saying, "It must be interesting for a young man/to have such a wise old fool for a lover" (*CP*, p. 232). Perhaps Goodman had earned the refrain to "Morning" (there is little else to it): "an ambiguous moralist/but my lust is authentic" (*CP*, p. 360).

Here I have been sketching a possible case for Goodman's poetry by stitching together bits of his two obsessive dilemmas: self-pitying megalomania and compulsive sex in conflict with his intellectuality. They may be really just one issue—the poet as sad grotesque, the self-conscious dirty-old-man, though one without the artful courage to more than scatter some rough fragments of his self-therapy.

There are a few other things in Goodman's hundreds of poems than the fractured documenting of his malaise. Some readers seem to think well of his rough-hewn imitations of late-Wordsworth,[64] though that may also constitute its own double condemnation. Something usually goes wrong with even his more suggestive efforts, such as the syntactical-sonnet-forcing of a poem of reflections upon a poem of reflections about "crazy Hudson," "Reading *Weepers Tower*" (*CP*, p. 213), whom he self-shockingly sees as paradigmatic of his aging obsessive self. Now and again lines struggle into suggestive metaphors, as in the Paul Klee–ish "ache-trees" where "small birds murmuring/ hop from twinge to twinge" (*CP*, p. 19). A very few even achieve a small poem, as with "Long Lines on the Left Bank," which ends, "Meaning is another world" (*CP*, p. 11). Some of the sexual laments cited above (such as "A Hustler" and "La Gaya Scienza," though not the more ambitiously long sets of verse catalogues such as the two "Lines to Mathew Ready") achieve an odd sort of awkward half-insight, as perhaps do several others, such as "Low Tide" (*CP*, p. 284), about ambiguously missed sexual possibility. A few Goodman gestures, however inadequately presented, are poignant in themselves, such as bringing a dandelion, bright and common, to the grave of his only son, killed at twenty in an accident (*CP*, p. 137). On that subject, too, he achieved one of his best little poems, the classical-imitation "For a Young Widow" (*CP*, p. 132),[65] who, in the good second stanza, is advised: "You see, girl, you ought not to / center your affections so, / little short of idolatry. / A young man is untrustworthy. / In the morning satisfied / he gets up from your bed/and in the evening he is dead."

But perhaps an archly folksy anarchist piece, with its mixture of resentment and sentiment, its beleaguered egotism and quatrains—and in spite of such dubious diction as "pretty" and "dignity"—would be the most suitable example to quote in full:

> Schultz, the neighbor's big black dog,
> used to shit on our scraggly lawn,
> but we feed him marrow bones
> and he treats our lawn like his home.
> The kids of Fulton Houses in New York
> smashed windows on our pretty block for spite;
> we gave them hockey sticks to play with
> and they smashed more windows.
> The dog is an anarchist like me,
> he has a careless dignity
> —that is, we never think about it,

which comes to the same thing.
The kids are political like you,
they want to win their dignity. They won't,
but maybe their children will be friendly dogs
and wag their tails with my grandchildren. (*CP*, pp. 360–61)

Not much else of Goodman's does as well, with its fracturing and incompetence, its stock form defeating his peculiarity in a stilted lack of the very plainness of fact and language that his own aesthetic demanded. Instead, he too "assiduously cultivated/ being depressed and the bawling inside me" (*CP*, p. 49) so that grossly egotistical compensations and pretensions resulted. It was perhaps less his peculiarity than his failure to allow it its own simple poetic reality which defeated him. Only fragments among the debris of his poetasting will do, and they mostly monument the failure of his hobby of obsessive writing in the attempts to have a literary life.

CHAPTER 5

Conclusion: The Libertarian Legacy

I Putting up the Headstone

PAUL Goodman's significance should not be confined to that of the failed litterateur —the bad novelist, story writer, dramatist, poet and belletrist. Literary history is often as weird and capricious as other histories, and so what the future will do with the two dozen volumes of literary remains I would not claim to know, though I have no doubt they are for the most part ruins, however one excavates them for good intentions or curious fragments or salutary lessons. One can find significant things in Goodman's artistic role-playing, but not much of it is literature.

Nor is Goodman, as I see him within the traditions, a major anarchist thinker, since he lacked the theoretical originality and rigor to suggest a broad libertarian view of social possibility and to confront its perplexities. As an anarchist, he was more suggestively earnest than deeply serious. However, maintaining a libertarian sense of things in uncongenial times was no mean achievement. Most importantly, Goodman should be of interest as a provocative libertarian social critic in the period from World War II through the American Vietnam War. This was not only as dissenter and anarchopacifist but for his insights and perspectives: on the new abolitionism of radically unschooling American education; on sexual freedom, especially for the young and homoerotic; on more meaningful places for youth and the marginal; on negating bureaucracy and power and domination in a technocracy; on considering possibilities of decentralized democratic community; and on other utopian responses to social evil. These had some influence and, I believe, retain considerable pertinence.

Goodman's impertinent claims to being a "genius" of all letters

144

and his self-conceit as artist-thinker might be understood not only as sad symptomology but as a muddled defense of his important libertarian role, even though he claimed the relation the other way around. When he asserted in one of his prefaces (as he had also in several verses), "I expect they'll put up a statue to me in the park" as an imaginative writer, it may appear as unintentional grotesque comedy. Let it be appropriate: twisted pebbled cement, iron rusting through, of an awkwardly squatting figure leaning on a pile of stone books—widespread mouth open, front tooth missing; pants fly also open—anonymously entitled *American Man of Letters*, and perhaps placed on an abandoned superhighway at the edge of a grassed-over New York City. But that might also be a fallacy of misplaced concreteness for one who obscurely sensed that he was keeping alive an important role and heritage, rather more important than himself, of the radical Man of Letters.

A better monument to a writer, I think, is a suitable and discriminating edition of his works. Certainly with Goodman a complete collected works could only be an embarrassing exposure before entombing (and another marker for the indiscriminate overproduction of current American academic scholarship). At first glance, Goodman's *oeuvre* appears large: including vanity press books, posthumous collections, and some still fugitive material as well as all the regularly published books, it would run around fifty volumes. However, cutting out the reprintings (with mostly only minor revisions) and repetitions, it would run about half that. Further eliminating the redundancies and trivia and very bad writing would more than halve that again. Goodman was not nearly as prolific as he appeared (as with his ostensible learning in many fields, that was rather more a role than a reality). After all, he spent much of his time talking and seducing and despairing and living the marginal life. A broadly tolerant selection might include half-a-dozen books, such as the revised edition of *Communitas*, the pamphlet *Drawing the Line*, the second half of *Gestalt Therapy*, *Utopian Essays*, *People or Personnel*, *Like a Conquered Province*, *New Reformation*. A more tough-minded selection might reasonably result in a moderate-sized one-volume anthology of properly edited-down and cleaned-up pieces. I suggest that this should

include no book complete, though I think a good half of Goodman's first, and still best, book of social criticism, *Communitas,*
could well go in. So could cut-and-pasted essays from each of
about four other volumes of social criticism: *Growing up Absurd*
(a short piece, with the clichés drastically reduced); an essay
on the argument for decentralizing made out of *People or Personnel*; a substantial piece on schooling/education, such as from
New Reformation (but certainly not the whole section, and with
bits drawn from his earlier educational tracts); several, perhaps
tightened-up, pieces from his miscellany volumes, *Utopian Essays*
and *Drawing the Line*; some excerpts from *Gestalt Therapy* and
Like a Conquered Province; and perhaps a couple of other pieces.
I hardly think a truly discriminating editor would include much
from the novels or any of the stories, though several of the travel
essays, such as "Our Visit to Niagara" and "A Statue of Goldsmith," might do. For literary criticism, since *belles lettres*—as
I have argued—gave Goodman much of his background and
self-definition, I would propose some excerpts from *Kafka's
Prayer* and a pieced-together essay for the main argument of
Speaking and Language. No responsible editor would include
anything from the plays. A handful of poems, plus a small scat-
tering of excerpts—as indicated in my discussion of the verse—
would fairly do. And a shrewd and hard-working editor could
include a catalogue-styled selection of jottings, notes, and varied
ruminations taken from a number of books (many of which I
have quoted), perhaps under the heading of "Pedantries and
Provocations."

In such a true anthology, there would also be room for several
memoirs, important since Goodman was a busy role-playing
public figure—one of him as Village *philosophe* aggressively laying on boys and girls at parties his erudition (a role at which
he played for about thirty years, sometimes strikingly), and
another profile of him as 1960s guru in the American hinterlands,
archly *outré* dissident at some campus conference, lecture and
postsession counseling-seduction. (I have not yet found any
such adequate memoirs.) While I hardly expect the prejudices
of likely editors and the exploitations of publishers and the
general crass dishonesty of the American book-business to produce such a one-volume anthology of Paul Goodman, it might

well be the proper monument to that eccentric writer, anarchist gadfly, libertarian social critic, and American literary radical.

II   *The Literary Radical*

Rightly to summarize Paul Goodman's significance might well require a "profile" of the type, the combined litterateur, social and cultural critic, engaged libertarian, and eccentric marginal personality—the American literary radical, subspecies of the Modern Western Intelligentsia. This Man of Letters would not be quite the highfalutin Renaissance humanist and Enlightenment artist whose mantles Goodman claimed, though recognizably a descendant, but rather the baggy-sweatered and stained-pants—and baggy-minded, stained ego—dissident, the endlessly argumentative *meshugena*. Intellectually more often a broker than originator, he takes large, peculiar ideas and styles as his quotidian labors, roughly repackaging them for broader use. His crude oddity should not obscure his services in transforming awareness and sensibility; his verbal manners may seem rusty saws, in contrast to the polished alloy instruments of more fully institutionalized culture mongers, but they may also provide the appropriate cutting edges of intellectual change. To the degree that we have an open culture—however arbitrary and fraudulently processed—such a bumptious mediator as this literary radical may not only contribute to it but personify it in his intensely taking it "seriously." Grant him the courage of his confusions.

I am suggesting that Paul Goodman's *role* as libertarian Man of Letters was quite probably more important than any of his specific works or ideas. Most essentially, his activity was contentious opinioning, "position-taking"—"Now look at what Paul Goodman is saying!" He served as an unusually earnest and impassioned taker of stances, defiant gestures, emphatic attitudes, on issues of concern, or should-be concern. He took on not just *an* issue of specialized knowledge or personal involvement but *all* issues that came up in his milieu (including many that I haven't discussed, such as how to play music, how to express anger, how to teach mathematics, how to frame modern paintings, and so on, in which personal ineptness was compen-

sated for with applied ideology). This was less a matter of great
intellectual learning and breadth (as awed naive readers seem
to think, though any well-informed person can see that Goodman didn't quite have it on his subject) than of self-defining
intellectual function. Fiction, city planning, sexology, poetry,
scientific organization, TV commercials, history, medicine, cos-
tuming, protest, psychotherapy, seating arrangements, education,
and the rest, were less his subjects than vehicles for ideological
opinions—varied occasions for performing as a radical intellectual.

No doubt partly aware of that, Goodman repeatedly down-
played his radicalism and costumed his ideologizing by talking
about the "practical." But an anarchist utopian can hardly pass
as moderate, any more than an intellectual ideologist can be
perceived as practical. Yet his partly disguised practice of
ideology was rather more peculiar and iconoclastic, and therefore more interesting, than most of the other "New York intellectuals" similarly engaged. To have a contentious opinion on
everything that comes to intellectual attention, as Goodman
usually did, arises less from art and learning than from an
anxiously energetic role in the purlieus of the cultural consensus

His "practicality" was that of the ideological dramaturgist. His
decent antagonism to the American Vietnam War or his dubious
patriotic mania for "space exploration" were less reasoned than
"struck," against official and intellectual fashion. They were
sincere, of course, but also served as dramatic position-takings.
Goodman's historically early, and antagonism-arousing, pronouncements on encouraging adolescent sexuality and on avoiding the draft were less thought-out views than importantly dissident gestures, which were also self-defining dissents from the
prevailing puritanic and "conscientious" radicalism. His arguments for decentralizing organizations and for abolishing compulsory schooling certainly had much justification, but they were
also high-styled defiances of usual social views. Goodman's
flaunting of homosexuality and bohemianism were hardly philosophical positons, though he draped some intellectual rags around
them, but rebellious personal demands which had a large social
visibility. His lifelong emphasis on the values of "community"
and "autonomy" certainly showed thought and imagination

(though not a subtle seriousness about their perplexities) but were most insistently cast as counters to our conditions of anomie and our atomizing ideologies. In context, his arguments, say, for eliminating all censoring restraints on mass media or for "banning cars" from the city were defiant fillips camouflaged as practical-sounding reforms. His woolly projections of autonomous neomedieval universities, or of Reichean psychotherapy for everyone, or of guilds of professionals practicing exalted ethics, were literally silly but understandable as part of a learned-naive dramaturgy of iconoclastic ideas. His prudent anarchism on public issues for liberal audiences, like his idiosyncratic neoclassicism on literary issues for vanguardist circles, served as provocative gestures as well as radical peculiarities.

Goodman was an ideologue, but, unlike most, such as Marxists and mystics, one with little taste for abstract entities, though, of course, he had all too much taste for overgeneralizing, whether on suburban life, medieval history, innate literary forms, or improbable social reforms. He must be understood as part of an ideological subculture which, in the past generation, frequently penetrated the mainline American culture, domesticating strange notions and sensibility. With more earnestness and principle, though with less imagination and panache than, say, Norman Mailer, he made broadly current certain radical opinions and impassioned responses which had previously been marginal.

In the longer run, Goodman would be a more persuasive figure if his works had had the tempered discipline of a more serious fictionist or critic (but a Malamud or a Trilling paid the price in self-limiting roles and ambiguous conservativism). The sophisticated can easily recognize the social-cultural genesis of Goodman's ideological role, just as the historically informed can recognize the sources of Goodman's not especially original literary, social-psychological and libertarian ideas. But his distinctive function was as a kind of "higher publicist" of the dissident communitarianism. The personal peculiarity and the ideological radicalism were probably essential to Goodman's gadfly role since, in fact, they were much of what he publicized and constitute much of his legacy.

Goodman was a major public practitioner of the art of "breakthrough" libertarianism. He was an anarchist not because he had a full-blown theory of a non-coercive society, of the ordering for freedom and equality, and of the ways of social revolution—little of which he had—but because he drew on the libertarian heritage and often attempted its essential responses. He rather more carried than created the black flag of an enduring and justified revolt that cannot be fully institutionalized. That is honorable and important intellectual work. His obviously bad writings and sometimes gross personality should not be used to deny this. Nor, of course, should they be ignored; hagiography here would be drastically falsifying and defeating. Through historical accident, and some opportunism as well as ideological persistence, Goodman became an important part of the Movement, the protest culture of the 1960s. With whatever mixed effects, that was a considerable contribution which carries into present dissatisfactions and dissents. As a portmanteau of dissident culture, he carried much that still needs unpacking, his libertarian insights as well as his many failures, some of which may be salutary.

Can an often bad writer and sloppy thinker and messy character do good intellectual work? Somewhat reluctantly, I must in the case of Paul Goodman anwer "yes." Since I have made the specific arguments in terms of various writings and issues, I offer a concluding broad suggestion. While we should recognize mixed and inadequate realities for what they are, those who find much of our world false and unfree will also recognize considerable value in Goodman's concerns and efforts. Even the cleverly half-disguised authoritarians and exploiters who dominate our culture and society might admit some need for such responses. And from whom else would the well-intentioned—"liberals" and the like—get many of their ideas to water, and water down? In our culture and society, we cannot interestingly survive without radical intellectuals, such as Paul Goodman, and the continuing services of the libertarian Man of Letters.

Notes and References

Chapter One

1. *Nature,* p. 239.

2. For example, he says he published some writing to make it "perfectly clear to everybody that I suck cocks." *Five Years* (New York, 1966), p. 249.

3. I am drawing on various personal reports and on such published memoirs as Leo Raditsa, "On Paul Goodman—and Goodmanism," *Iowa Review* 5(Summer 1974), 1–18; Richard Kostelantz, *Master Minds* (New York, 1969), pp. 97–121; Alfred Kazin, "The Girl from the Village," *Atlantic* 227(Feb. 1971), 57–63; George Dennison, "A Memoir and Appreciation," Goodman *CP,* pp. xiii–xxx.

4. *Five Years,* pp. 85, 150; *Speaking* (New York, 1971), p. 235.

5. *Five Years,* p. 9. Robert Mazzocco explains Goodman's social earnestness as "anxiety over identity becomes anxiety about the world." *New York Review of Books,* 14(May 21, 1970), pp. 3–4.

6. Alfred Kazin, *New York Jew* (New York, 1978), pp. 45, 93. While Kazin is often imperceptive, other sources confirm these points. For example, see the earlier descriptions of Delmore Schwartz in a stiffly written but intelligent satire on the Goodman coterie, *The World Is a Wedding* (New York, 1948), pp. 9–68. See also James Atlas, *Delmore Schwartz* (New York, 1977), pp. 59 ff.

7. *Five Years,* p. 25.

8. *Words* (New York, 1964), p. 19.

9. *Parents' Day* (Saugatuck, Conn., 1951), p. 154.

10. *Nature,* pp. 231, 228.

11. "On Being a Writer . . . ," in *Nature,* p. 209. In posthumously published ramblings, "Thoughts on Fever . . . ," he notes rather smugly that he took up literature out of a "fear of competing" and of making an "adult adjustment." *New Letters* 42(Winter/Spring 1976), 191–94. For ineptness, see *New Reformation* (New York, 1970), p. 201.

12. *Parents' Day;* p. 176.

13. *Little Prayers and Finite Experience* (New York, 1972), p. 27.

14. For some of the rather uninsightful claims, see "The Politics

of Being Queer," *Nature*, pp. 216–25. He also claims that his homo-sexuality inspired his libertarian sense of humanity. *New Reformation*, p. 194. Also, a sense of beauty and democracy. *Nature*, p. 217. His sexuality may have been a bit above average: "There have been few days back to my 11th year when I have not had an orgasm one way or another." *Five Years*, p. 247. Bisexuality, of course, allowed more varied opportunities. He also grants that his sexuality was an "obsession" similar to a false cult religion. *Five Years*, p. 164. He claims that he was "lofty-minded" as a "reward" for his "abject sexuality" (p. 87). But see Ch. 4, below.

15. I am not competent to discuss Goodman's interest in music. The composer-devotee he often worked with thought he was a great poet—"my Goethe, my Blake, and my Appollinaire"—but that his music was "technically childlike" and "any well-trained non-entity could have done better." Ned Rorem, *Pure Contraption* (New York, 1974), pp. 98–100. For a listing of Goodman's lyrics, see Rorem's *Music and People* (New York, 1968).

16. Emphasized by respondents, but see also Ch. 3, below.

17. He must use it several dozen times; the earliest I recall (1946?) is in *The Empire City* (New York, 1959), p. 240.

18. See *Five Years*, p. 41; *Nature*, p. 237; and scattered remarks in *New Reformation*, *Speaking*, and *Little Prayers*.

19. For one instance, see his saying (ca. 1960) that he doesn't know anyone who supports Kennedy or Nixon, who doesn't think all TV programming is "trash," and who makes "war talk." *Society*, p. 157. Part of this was earlier Jewish separateness from mainstream America—its saving grace, according to Goodman, "but the subur-banite Jews have sunk into spiritual degradation." *Five Years*, p. 227.

20. See Irving Howe, "The New York Intellectuals," *Decline of the New* (New York, 1970), pp. 211–65, which passingly discusses Goodman with his generation's view of "the writer as dilettante-connoisseur, *Luftmensch* of the mind, roamer among theories."

21. On the *PR* issue, see Howe, above, and Taylor Stoehr, *Line*, pp. xiv ff., who, however, takes it too seriously. For *Politics*, see Richard King, *The Party of Eros* (Chapel Hill, N. C., 1972), pp. 31 ff.; MacDonald said he had promoted Goodman in spite of many readers' objections (personal conversation, 1977). Several of Good-man's eight contributions display the New York parochialism, as with denying anything distinctively American to the broader culture: "The Attempt to Invent an American Style," *Politics* 1 (Feb. 1944), 17–18.

22. *Making It* (New York, 1967), pp. 296 ff.

23. For a fashion mongering blurb, see Theodore Solotaroff, *The*

Red Hot Vacuum (New York, 1970), pp. 211–16; for an over-praiser gone successful and righteously sour, see Joseph Epstein, "Paul Goodman in Retrospect," *Commentary* 65(Feb. 1978), 70–73; for burbly claims for an "incandescent Socratic figure," see Morris Dickstein, *Gates of Eden* (New York, 1977), pp. 74–80; more qualified, George Steiner, "On Paul Goodman," *Commentary* 36(Aug. 1963), 158–63. None is well-informed.

24. See my "The End of Criticism," *Praxis* 1(Spring 1975).

25. See Stoehr, *Creator*, pp. xii ff. Goodman had earlier published a few verses and, drawing on his brother, some comments on architecture. As his first social philosophising, he shortly later published some indecisively clever, and unradical, ruminations, "The Moral Idea of Money," *Journal of Philosophy* 32(1935), 126–31.

26. "The Politics of Being Queer," *Nature,* p. 217.

27. Later he views Falstaff as "the most aesthetically realized character," but Shakespeare "deceived himself" about his own values. *Speaking,* p. 85.

28. (New York, 1947). He rebuts Kafka's suffering with Spinoza's line "Happiness is not the reward of virtue, it is itself a virtue."

29. See *Absurd,* pp. 170 ff., and Appendix E, pp. 279 ff. See my "The Beat in the Rise of the Populist Culture," *The Thirties,* ed. Warren French (Deland, Fla., 1967).

30. See the thin "Wordsworth's Poems" (1969), *Creator,* pp. 51–5.

31. *Utopian,* pp. 236–53. For contrast, see the Abingdon Bible commentaries. There are also many odds and ends of literary criticism which don't merit much discussion.

32. He gives various excuses for his bad writing (as on p. 38), blaming subject or audience. Linguistic imperceptivity may have been part of the problem since he thought strong emotion led to good speech (p. 52), as did earnestness (p. 46), when the opposite is more often true, and that slang was verbal nonconformity (p. 67) instead of the opposite. His comments on grammar (pp. 91 ff.) also seem dubious. As to his citing himself several dozen times in this book, perhaps it is explained elsewhere: "I have become my own classic text." *Five Years,* p. 135. He found his earlier lack of fame absurd (p. 85).

33. Goodman seems to still be fighting with philosophical positivists of an earlier generation (Stevenson, Ayers, and the like) who divided language into the "emotive" and theirs: "Emotions do not necessarily hinder knowing" because "all emotions have a cognitive part; they say something about the environment in relation to the self"; on "Darwinian grounds we would not have them if they had

not proved useful for survival." *Speaking*, p. 146. Elsewhere, he notes that language "is not a game with conventional rules, for it is an engaged behavior, a way of being in the world." *Five Years*, p. 88. One can sympathize while recognizing his weak case.

34. *New Reformation*, p. 117.

35. His one extended example is a thin stylistic analysis of bits of *The Sun Also Rises* (pp. 181 ff.), not up to the standard in the field (Earl Rovit, Jackson Benson, R. P. Warren) because he can't grant, much less abide, Hemingway's essential stoicism.

36. I am ignoring here his personal "Notes for a Defence of Poetry" since I take up his muddled poetics in terms of his poems, below.

37. Another version appears in the preface to *Utopian* a decade earlier. Essentially, he makes an antiacademic case for amateurism and broad responsiveness. "A man of letters finds that the nature of things is not easily divided into disciplines." *Little Prayers*, p. 43.

38. He was, of course, predisposed to social criticism by character and milieu. In literature, he was predisposed to moralistic putdowns, as in comically claiming that Henry Miller and similar writers lacked "edification." *Absurd*, p. 215.

Chapter Two

1. Alfred Kazin identifies Goodman as an ex-Trotskyite in the 1940s, perhaps on the basis of some bad verses entitled "The Death of Trotsky" (*CP*, pp. 32–6). *Atlantic* 227(Feb. 1971), 62. But I find no evidence of it.

2. *Making Do* (New York, 1963), p. 152.

3. See Renato Poggioli, *The Theory of the Avant-Garde* (Cambridge, Mass., 1968). For the Cynics, see Chapter One of my *Literary Rebel*. A standard history of anarchism is George Woodcock, *Anarchism* (New York, 1962). For brief accounts of contemporary anarchism, see my "Anarchism Revived," *Nation* 211(Nov. 16, 1970); and "In Praise of Anarchism," *Village Voice* (Feb. 16, 1973). For current anarchism, see *Reinventing Anarchy*, ed. H. and C. Ehrlich, et al. (London, 1979). Goodman frequently cites Kropotkin, *Mutual Aid* and *Factories and Fields*, and he wrote a brief praising piece around *Memoirs of a Revolutionist*: "Kropotkin at the Moment," *Dissent* 15 (Nov.-Dec. 1968), 519–22. But other references to libertarian writings are cursory: Tolstoy once, several vague references to Baukunin, a very brief review of several histories of

the movement—"The Anarchists," *Liberation* 10 (June–July 1965), 10—typically dismissive references to such individualists as Thoreau —*People*, p. 39. His late introduction to a reprint of Alexander Berkman, *Prison Memoirs of an Anarchist* (New York, 1970) [unpaginated] rather patronizingly treats him as too idealistic. Goodman's remarks on prisons are silly, though elsewhere he suggested that they were inevitable for some and so should be made as painless as possible—*Little Prayers*, p. 53.

4. One of them, David Wieck, in a long thin review-essay, has recently discussed Goodman's anarchism, emphasizing that it derived from World War II pacifism, from Kantian ethics, from bits of Enlightenment philosophy, from the Rousseauistic side of psychoanalysis, from a one-sided interpretation of Jefferson, and (dubiously) from his aesthetics. He also notes that it was often closer to liberalism than radicalism, lacked concern with justice, feminism, and other libertarian goals, but continued the main tradition. *Telos* (Spring 1978), 199–214.

5. In *Art and Social Nature* (New York, 1946). I have quoted the slightly variant versions reprinted in *Line*.

6. Some of the various and contradictory uses of "nature" also appear in a novel of this period, *The State of Nature* (part of *The Empire City*, discussed in Ch. 4). Richard King points out that Goodman's use of "nature" not only is question-begging but stock "naturalistic fallacy" in the "equation of the natural with the good and the healthy." *Party of Eros* (Chapel Hill, N.C., 1972), p. 94. True, but Goodman's use of "nature" is sometimes clear in context, and he does accept some negative qualities of "nature."

7. And which, of course, accounts for one of the contemporary uses of "anarchist" applied, wrongly, to the West German Baeder-Meinhoff and other extremist groups. But if radical history has shown that some rebels are "psychopaths," it is even truer that often "the lawgiver *is* a psychopathic personality" trying to contain his own conflicts. *Five Years*, p. 78.

8. As Colin Ward points out, "What some people have found unique about his preoccupations is not really . . . they are the characteristics of the anarchist approach. . . ." "The Anarchist as Citizen," *New Letters* 42(Winter/Spring 1976), p. 239. He rightly emphasizes Goodman's commitment to "autonomy" among traditional anarchist themes. He also notes his "amazing infelicities of language," his insular views, and his lack of understanding of the issues of women, minorities and workers, 237–45. But he is sympa-

thetic to Goodman; see *Anarchy in Action* (New York, 1973), which is also dedicated to Goodman.

9. At this level, Goodman was a far more commonsensical left-Freudian than Norman O. Brown or Herbert Marcuse, though of course he shows little of the poetic and metapsychological dialectics of *Life Against Death* and *Eros and Civilization*.

10. For the more technical arguments against majoritarian and representative concepts, see Robert Paul Wolff, *In Defense of Anarchism* (New York, 1970). But perhaps it is less questions of principle than of magic and prejudice in our meritocracy, since random selection would usually seem both more just and meritorious, whether in conscription, elite school admission, or bureaucratic authority.

11. It is not clear to me why "social initiative" was so important to Goodman; a later example: "A major means of creating an effective pluralism is decentralization, to increase the amount of mind and the number of wills initiating and deciding." *Province*, p. 132. It seems quantitative, as if more mind and will were equatable with free, better.

12. *Kafka's Prayer* (New York, 1947), p. 18.

13. I am using the "revised" edition here (New York, 1960). Apparently the work was first written in the early 1940s, revised in 1946 (Chicago, 1947). The later revision included some rearrangement, minor updating with materials on highways, additional examples of a Chinese commune and Black Mountain College, and a greater emphasis on "affluence." A few awkward paragraphs were dropped and the conclusion was made less personal and condensed. Appendixes are the same. In essentials, the work was little changed. Though well-known, *Communitas* seems to have had little published discussion. The longest is by David Riesman, "Some Observations on Community Plans and Utopia," *Individualism Reconsidered* (Glencoe, Ill., 1954), pp. 70–98. A broad but bland defense of utopianism, it is positive toward *Communitas* but notes its dependence on Mumford, the unfairness to Howard, perhaps overrates the relevance of the Bellamy tradition, and properly makes a point about the cursory history in the book.

14. Curiously, Goodman's comments on Fuller some years later reversed into praise, with little justification. *New Reformation*, p. 31.

15. For identification of several of the later issues, see my "Professors and Communes," *AAUP Bulletin* (Dec. 1974).

16. Later, but not here, he refers to Paradigm II as illustrating "an anarcho-syndicalist principle," though he then substitutes a meliorist approach to the rural-urban imbalance. *Province*, p. 88. His

bohemian hatred of suburbs remained constant: "I think suburbs ought to be wiped out." *Line*, p. 263. He saw them as aggregates rather than communities, and he rather Platonically held that a "community is not the sum of individuals." *Five Years*, p. 245.

17. An earlier version of some of this appeared in *Politics* (1944), reprinted in *Line*, pp. 48–54, which made a point of adding to function and humane purpose the "playful freedom" of art.

18. Some years later Goodman defends his scheme against the guaranteed income advocates (Robert Theobald and others), though further on he partly agrees with them. *People*, pp. 119, 167 ff.

19. As King rightly says, *Communitas* is "a work full of fertile suggestions" but "assumes that community is in itself a positive value." Obviously, community can be quite bad. Perhaps more problematic: "Goodman's linking of self-regulation and mutual aid is not at all convincing . . . as unsatisfactory as the 'invisible hand' solution was in capitalist ideology." *Party of Eros*, pp. 91–93.

20. First published in *Anarchy* (London) 62 (April 1966), reprinted in *Line*, pp. 176–77.

21. Originally a Smithsonian lecture; *Line*, pp. 55–66.

22. See also the lucid lecture "Urbanization and Rural Reconstruction," *Province*, pp. 77–97, partly repeated in *New Reformation*, pp. 184 ff. He is inconsistent, often, on overpopulation, sometimes dismissing it as a liberal-elitist issue, though it obviously is crucial to libertarianism. See *Line*, p. 263.

23. Contrary to much evidence, he thinks small profit-making is usually benign (p. 8), but no doubt it depends on the conditions. Elsewhere, he makes a profound but undeveloped insight: "The tolerable background for any economic activity cannot be an object of economic activity." *Little Prayers*, p. 65. Market freedom requires a prior community, and its restraints. He does not explain why he accepts disparities of wealth (p. 75).

24. He does admit that decentralizing would not guarantee quality (p. 87), and that bureaucratic procedures often do protect against "arbitrary injustice" (p. 88)—a main impetus to them, I think.

25. For the peripheral relevance of small dependent countries, see Barrington Moore, Jr., *The Social Origins of Dictatorship and Democracy* (Boston, 1966). Goodman often uses the example, as in *Province*, pp. 96–97.

26. I have mostly ignored his capsulated American history, such as "the effort of the Populists is beyond praise" (p. 43) in furthering our best pragmatism and progressivism of industrial democracy. It looks to me as if he is drawing on Norman Pollack, *The Populist*

Response to Industrial America (Cambridge, Mass., 1962)—and perhaps Walter Nugent—in fervently rejecting prevalent liberal negations of such movements, such as by Richard Hofstader and others. From recent literature on the subject, such as Lawrence Goodman, *Democratic Promise: The Populist Movement in America* (New York, 1976), he may have been loosely aiming in the right direction. Populist becomes a magical name for him in his later writings. However, much of his historicizing tends to dogmatic simplifications. In "A Conjecture in American History, 1783–1815," *Politics* 6(Winter 1949), 11–12, he proposed that the early republic was a "quasi-anarchistic society." Though Richard Hofstader and Oscar Handlin, on the following pages, raise serious qualifications, Goodman repeats the essential argument, no longer a "conjecture," in *People* and elsewhere. The claimed libertarianism of a United States committed to drastic inequalities, pathological religion, slavery, and genocide, seems to be patriot-distortion.

27. I suppose that Goodman has in mind the sociological apologetics of Seymour Lipset, Daniel Bell, and the like. Stock criticism of lack of his practicality is given by Michael Harrington, *Atlantic*, 216 (August 1965), 88–91.

28. *Province*, p. 140. With this goes a great faith in rational co-operativeness. See *Line*, p. 209.

29. The negative analysis of campus rebels is in *New Reformation*, pp. 49–63; for the libertarian-Leninist contrast, see "The Black Flag of Anarchism," *Line*, p. 207. For other views on student rebels, see my "Revolution Before Noon?" *Village Voice* (April 6, 1972), and Chapter 9 of the *End of Culture* (San Diego, 1975).

30. For example, note the switch in Herbert Marcuse's views from *An Essay on Liberation* (Boston, 1969) to *Counter-Revolution and Revolt* (Boston, 1972).

31. For the other emphasis, see *American Radical Thought: The Libertarian Tradition*, ed, H. J. Silverman (Lexington, Mass., 1970).

32. See also Goodman's "The Diggers in 1984," *Ramparts* 6(Sept. 1967), 28–30—a combination of futurism and harangue—and Emmett Grogan, *Ringolevio: A Life Played for Keeps* (Boston, 1972). Goodman dubiously Kropotkinizes such rebels.

33. Reprinted in *Line*, p. 215 ff. Since many desired reforms require centralizing, in spite of the need for decentralizing, he admits "there is real confusion here, shared by myself," p. 219.

34. For Goodman's contradictory view of science, see Ch. 3. He seems contradictory on the Protestant work ethic, also, agreeing it must be rejected by the "new reformation," but defending it, above,

and elsewhere arguing that if Americans were free many would rightly not work: "Our Standard of Living," *Line*, p. 250.

35. Anarchism, I think, must deny any sovereignty in principle, though of course, prudently reckon with it, like nasty weather, in practical circumstances. But Goodman frequently vacillates, as with populist sovereignty, in "Anarchism and Revolution," *Line*, p. 229.

36. In *Line*, p. 208. "The danger is not in loosening the machine but in its tightening up by panic repression" (p. 225). Earlier, parodying Proudhon, he rightly suggested in a symposium that "order is chaos" because its imposition makes "explosion inevitable," and authoritarian imposition produces "the harmony of the graveyard," *Freedom and Order in the University*, ed. S. Gerovitz (Cleveland, 1967), p. 34. He later suggests the wise argument that democracy is good because it is weak, thus not allowing full exercise of evil power (p. 56).

37. Goodman shows several positions on the good/evil of human nature. Early, he usually asserts "natural" goodness; when people aren't "good," he follows the favored American correlative, the frustration-hypothesis—"the corruptability of mankind is caused by frustration," *Line*, p. 255. But, especially later, men may be naturally bad—indeed, they have "a right to be crazy, stupid, or arrogant," *Little Prayers*, p. 45—and so we better minimize their power to coerce others and be corrupt or destructive. The optimistic and pessimistic can both be libertarian (in spite of nonsense propounded by conservatives), but the first will emphasize community, and the latter protection from it.

38. Better was the temporary view some years earlier: "One is not giving up Western values if one suggests that in present circumstances it would be wise to give up the United States of America." *Society*, p. 54. "The anarchist position is not a doctrinaire position of no government" but "a continual tendency to try to increase autonomy." Thus the American "Bill of Rights is an anarchist document." *Freedom and Order*, p. 156. But he shrewdly notes later: "The weakness of my anarchism is that the lust for freedom is a powerful motive for political change, whereas autonomy is not." *Little Prayers*, p. 47. Oftentimes he escaped into irrationalist optimism—we should act on freedom but not formulate it or it becomes restrictive. See the awkward little ruminations, "The Formulation of Freedom," *New Letters* (Winter/Spring 1976), 145–50.

Chapter   Three

1. *CP,* p. 104. Stoehr also uncritically argues that he saw his literary work as "therapeutic." "Adam and Everyman: Paul Goodman in His Stories," *Salmagundi* 38–39(Summer-Fall 1977), 137–50. For an opposite extreme view, see Lewis S. Feurer's obsessional treatment of youth rebellion as pathological and Goodman as one of its "fixated" manipulators in his pursuit of "homosexual power needs" in *The Conflict of Generations* (New York, 1969). But see my "Father and Son Destroyers," *Nation* 208(May 5, 1969). For an example of incoherent criticism, see Daniel Rosenblatt, "The Demonology of the Superego," *Commentary* 29(June 1960), 520–32, with reply by Goodman, 532–4.

2. Some details about *Absurd* being rejected and then accepted by the publisher are given by Norman Podhoretz, *Making It* (New York, 1967), pp. 296 ff. One of the better reviews was a curmudgeonly but perceptive long one by John J. Enck, who saw *Absurd* as superficial and clichéd, weakened also by "aggressive idiosyncrasies" and bad writing. *Wisconsin Studies in Contemporary Literature* 1(Fall 1960), 89–103.

3. For the personal motivation, see: "In God's creation, I'm a kind of juvenile delinquent." *Five Years,* p. 62. He also acknowledged that writing on youth was his way of "living out my missed adolescence," p. 221.

4. For Goodman the issues are also not Marxian social class; he fears extreme class disparity (p. 59) but it is not central to him.

5. Of the "hipsterism" of the time, he attributes it to Mailer, and similar figures, and calls it an unrebellious version of competitive role playing, p. 91.

6. In a suggestive essay, he notes that the middle-class obsession with family psychologising is a mark of social deprivation, as is the "Lear-complex" of abnegating to the young. "The Children and Psychology," *Nature,* pp. 93–9.

7. His later view suggests resignation in bad marriages. *New Reformation,* p. 192.

8. His cures for youthful delinquency: replace "violent sex" by "guiltless sex," "defiance" by "real enemies," and "foolish actionism" by "worthwhile tasks" *Society,* p. 163.

9. *Utopian,* pp. 252–62. The next two lectures discussed are also in this collection, as is a weak one on the primarily secular concerns of religious groups, "Post-Christian Man."

10. *Line,* pp. 127–41.

11. *Little Prayers*, p. 27; *Line*, p. 129. Earlier: "The university is lousy, but it is all there is." *Five Years*, p. 249.

12. *Line*, p. 244.

13. Among those acknowledging his influence, see: George Dennison, *The Lives of Children* (New York, 1969); the editors, Ronald and Beatrice Gross, *Radical School Reform* (New York, 1969); I. L. Gotz, ed., *No Schools* (New York, 1971); John Holt, *Freedom and Beyond* (New York, 1972), and *Escape from Childhood* (New York, 1974); Everett Reimer, *School is Dead* (Garden City, N. Y., 1971); Ivan Illich, who wrote "Goodman most radically obliged me to revise my thinking," *De-Schooling Society* (New York, 1972). Some are more ambiguous, such as Edgar Z. Friedenberg, who vaguely said Goodman was an "untidy writer" who was usually right. *New York Review of Books* 3(Nov. 19, 1964).

14. Perhaps important to his later negative view was his rejection by even a "progressive" college. Martin Duberman, *Black Mountain* (New York, 1972), pp. 330–3, blamed it on his extreme righteousness about his bisexuality. Goodman (in conversation) blamed it on bigotry against his casual style. One knowing respondent claimed it was the usual academic battle of egos which got him dropped.

15. See "From John Dewey to A. S. Neill," *Seeds of Liberation*, ed. Paul Goodman (New York, 1964); and *New Reformation*, pp. 82–3, where he suggests rebellious students were carrying out the ethos of "progressive education," though much ended up as technocracy and suburban conformity. *Line*, p. 75. See also *Absurd*, pp 78–86, for admission that Deweyism weakened the humanities and ended in "adjustment" indoctrination. For "youth," see *New Reformation*, p. 85.

16. *Scholars*, pp. 74, 63.

17. See *Freedom and Order in the University*, pp. 31–56. The bureaucratic-mindedness of the academics in this symposium tends to confirm Goodman's arguments.

18. See "The Freedom to Be Academic" (1956), appended to *Absurd*, p. 278. He questions the "norm of neutrality," the failure to speak out on many important issues, and, as a libertarian, shows little patience with either liberal anxiety or timidity about 1950s anti-Communism.

19. *New Reformation*, p. 75; *Line*, p. 71.

20. *Scholars*, p. 4; *Line*, passim.

21. *Line*, p. 80.

22. *Line*, p. 69. The best of culture is learned by self-discovery. "By separating 'learning' from real-life functions and assigning it to

schools, we get a host of artificial problems about learning and schools, and indeed inhibit learning." Over-schooling is essentially a vicious cop-out from the "social problems" of access, real work, institutional democracy, and so on. "The Relation of Culture and Learning," *Canadian Psychologist* 13(1972), 304.

23. *New Reformation*, p. 116.

24. *Absurd*, p. 146. On science best not learned in schools, see *Compulsory*, pp. 117–23. But he doesn't consider the equal corruptions, and lesser autonomy, elsewhere.

25. *Scholars*, p. 30.

26. *New Reformation*, p. 68. The end of rioting, pacified by several kinds of doping, has not, of course, changed the issues.

27. *Scholars*, p. 8.

28. *Compulsory*, p. 154.

29. This is not intended to refute his charges, nor his description of the "academic personality" and its sycophancy, trivial publishing, time-serving, tenured mediocrity, antiintellectualism, and so on— "the worst possible expense of spirit in a waste of shame," processing in servility. *Scholars*, pp. 84–106. For my qualifications, see *End of Culture*.

30. His "Reforms and Proposals," *Scholars*, pp. 131 ff., all run against the system. His "not to spend one penny more . . . by present School administrators," *Freedom and Order*, p. 39, points of course beyond reformism. Also, *Compulsory*, p. 73.

31. *Scholars*, p. 168. But as Christopher Jencks rightly noted, "Goodman does not take his own proposals seriously enough to examine even their most obvious consequences," such as what would happen to intellectual quality. *New Republic*, 14 (Nov. 16, 1962), 24. Certainly many intellectual faculty—admittedly, a small minority itself—would, because of individuality and unfashionableness, be excluded from these academic communities. But Jencks is unserious in ignoring the other issues and criticisms.

32. I am drawing on my own experiences in the 1960s. For a more positive account, see Paul Lauter and Florence Howe, *The Conspiracy of the Young* (New York, 1970), pp. 79-126.

33. *New Reformation*, p. 103.

34. *Line*, p. 270.

35. *New Reformation*, p. 67.

36. *Line*, p. 242. See also *Mass Education in Science* (Los Angeles, 1966), p. 16. As to writing, schools create "the wooden attitude." *Compulsory*, p. 33.

37. *New Reformation*, p. 77.

38. *Absurd*, p. 24.

39. In *Nature*, p. 97.

40. *Scholars*, p. 109.

41. *Gestalt Therapy* (New York, 1951), p. 343.

42. Teaching machines are uneducational in principle because they try to prestructure "a kind of behavior, learning, that can be discriminating, graceful, and energetic only if the organism itself creates its own structure as it goes along." *New Reformation*, p. 76. Essentially similar arguments are applied by Goodman against "cognitive development," specifically criticizing Jerome Bruner—and by implication the later work of Piaget. Libertarianized Kantianism?

43. *Compulsory*, p. 173.

44. *Line*, p. 77; *New Reformation*, p. 87. "Probably there are half a dozen well-marked types of learning." *Freedom and Order*, p. 36.

45. I comment on several of these elsewhere. See also *Kafka's Prayer* (New York, 1947), p. 136, where he argues that, to avoid Kafkaesque family relations, children need more autonomy and wider community. See also *New Reformation*, p. 87. He makes the obvious attacks on credentialing for jobs, though not on what I consider one of its worst aspects, hierarchicalism (so nurses don't become doctors; mechanics, engineers; clerks, managers; and so on).

46. *Line*, pp. 78–80.

47. *Line*, p. 67.

48. *Line*, p. 68; *New Reformation*, p. 85.

49. *New Reformation*, p. 88.

50. Also: "One has the impression that our social psychologists are looking not to a human community but to a future in which the obsessionals will take care of the impulsives." *Compulsory*, p. 27. And: much of the academic approach to social problems "confirms the inequitable structure of the economy," p. 72. As to ethnic "minority" issues, he has Enlightenment distaste to "Bussing," "open enrollment," etc., and so ends in reluctant liberal acceptance. *Society*, p. 183. There is a disturbing smugness to his dismissals of some issues; for example, "Students who must learn will always get the money to pay for their learning." *Scholars*, p. 27. As one who tried that puritanic route, and ended up ill as well as ill-educated, I am not persuaded.

51. This was the position he took as member of a local New York School Board in the early 1960s; letters and statements on it are scattered through *Society*. He was also involved with a Summerhill-

type school and with the one described by Dennison in *The Lives of Children*.

52. *Compulsory*, p. 42.

53. Only libertarians, right-wing as well as anarchist, seem to object to compulsory schooling—see Holt and Illich, cited above. In some loose ruminations on cats, dogs, and children in the city for a book of rather trite photographs by Stefan Congrat-Butlar, Goodman puts a favorite point: if by schooling and other confines we inhibit "the spontaneity of children, it will return as stupidity, gracelessness, and violent crime." *The Open Look* (New York, 1969), [no pagination—11 pp. by Goodman].

54. *Scholars*, p. 48.

55. The praise of Faraday as a cynosure of the self-made scientist is in *Little Prayers*.

56. He would not give grants to large research projects but to tens of thousands of nonprofessional tinkerers in the belief that true ingenuity and initiative come from the eccentric (p. 64). Again, he doesn't seem to be aware of the revolutionary implications, which would be to abolish modern science.

57. The language here partly disguises the extremity of the demand, a religious call for near-saintly, austere virtues for technologues, a reformation sermon for purification of the scientific priesthood. See *Little Prayers*, p. 71.

58. Again, suggestive but unserious. Look at his "Seating Arrangements" essay, *Utopian*, pp. 156–81. While he is perceptive in asking what are the implications of various groupings (churches, eating) he doesn't follow through (experimental theater, buffet dining). If "the analysis of a seating plan soon involves us in central considerations of theology, of political and medical theory, of poetics, of community mores," how much more complex subtlety would be needed for science and technology?

59. *Utopian*, pp, 145–55.

60. *Line*, pp. 99–103; the others: *New Republic* 148 (Jan. 26; Feb. 23; Mar. 16; Mar. 30; Apr. 13; Apr. 20; May 25; June 8— 1963). Editing may have improved his writing. He argues that TV is hopelessly dominated by ads, suburban socialization, pseudointellectuality even in "serious" formats, anxious stupidity, and crass corporate control; he proposes decommercializing, decentralizing, abolition of networks, more open formats, and that "we would be better off if TV did not exist." For good observations on TV's effects, see "Format and Anxiety," *Society*, pp. 26–35. Though limited, he is better on TV than on films, on which he earlier practiced a rather

smug aesthetic. See *Partisan Review* 7(1940), 45 ff.; 8(May-June 1941), 237 ff.; 9 (Mar.-April 1942), 141 ff.—on Chaplin, Griffiths, and the shape of the screen. He also had done some slight pieces on cinema for the periodical *Trend* (1934–35).

61. "The Chance for Popular Culture" (1949), *Creator,* pp. 79–87. See my "Sensibility Under Technocracy," *Human Connection and the New Media,* ed. Barry Schwartz (Englewood Cliffs, N. J., 1973).

62. "New Theatre and the Unions," *Creator,* pp. 123–31.

63. "A New Deal for the Arts," *Creator.*

64. See the scattered slighting remarks in *New Reformation* and contrast my "The Rebellious Culture," *Sociological Essays,* ed. Charles Anderson (Homewood, Ill., 1974) and "The Electric Aesthetic and the Short-Circuit Ethic," *Mass Culture Revisited,* ed. D. M. White and B. Rosenberg (New York, 1971).

65. Moral legislation, he reasonably argues, tries to get calculated response from compulsive behavior not open to such suasion. *Little Prayers,* p. 53.

66. I detect other Goodman sources to include Taoism, American literary naturalism, Kropotkin, stock Greek mythology, Buber, the "frustration—aggression hypothesis" (Dollard), and Deweyean instrumentalism.

67. Though you would never know it from reading Mailer, Marcuse, Brown, or most learned accounts of them.

68. In a 1945 review of Reich, he saw him as a "narrow and even inhumane" thinker, though good for encouraging sexual freedom. *Nature,* pp. 75–8. See also "Great Pioneer But No Libertarian," *Nature,* pp. 81–6. Goodman reports that his advocacy was rejected by Reich (who I think had been mad since the 1930s). For contrasting view, see Don Calhoun, *Liberation* 3(Jan. 1958), on whose unpublished "Psychology of Subordination" I also draw on below. Goodman criticizes Reich's "orgone energy" and other positivism in *Gestalt Therapy* (p. 393), insisting (like Pierre in *War and Peace*) that if the magical force existed it would still have to be part of "ordinary assimilation and growth."

70. See Stoehr's preface to *Nature,* pp. ix–xxiv. In a breezy anecdotal biography, Martin Shepard's *Fritz* (New York, 1975), Perls is credited with the name of the movement and the originating outline of the book (p. 63). Though Perls was the more astute therapist, Goodman's domination of the early movement, including training and conference activities, partly depended on his role-playing art-coterie leader (p. 57). My anecdotal information is that Goodman was an eccentric therapist with homosexual obsessions and hostilities.

71. Forgetting his Freud, Goodman smugly claimed that examples belonged in novels (p. 460); his few specific touches are farcical, such as metaphoric distinctions of red anger, white fury, purple rage (p. 344).

72. And insistent hostility based, he said, in Jewishness, and which may help explain his savaging Hemingway, Protestantism, existentialism and similar alien views.

73. In "My Psychology as a 'Utopian Sociologist,'" he admits he was "not serious about most people's *actual* plight in the world." *Nature*, p. 227.

74. In contrast to some sexologues, Goodman had a limited sense of possibility; in what I take to be a jab at Norman Mailer, he wrote that the "idea of the apocalyptic orgasm is pure epilepsy." "Sex and Ethics," *Nature*, p. 116. Mailer jabbed back in *Armies of the Night* (1968) by mocking Goodman's bad writing and obstreperous personality. Incidentally, note that while Goodman favors masturbation, he lists four bad ways of doing it. *Nature*, p. 107. New puritanism?

75. See "A Public Dream of Universal Disaster," *Nature*, p. 92. But he simple-mindedly views the army as satisfying sado-masochism, which shows little sense of the bureaucratized military.

76. "In America, there is entirely too much preoccupation with being 'mature' once and for all; but this prevents continuing growth . . . and a fuller maturity." *Society*, p. 81. Other anti-Freudianism: the love of children makes no demands, has no resentment, produces no guilt. *Little Prayers*, p. 99. That dissolves the family drama.

77. "What is called 'sublimation' is a direct but imperfect satisfaction of the same need." *Gestalt Therapy*, p. 443. He often seemed to hold that frustration simply produces aggression. For a libertarian critique of that notion, see my "Towards a Politics for *Homo Negans*: Reflections On Human Aggression," *Personalist* 53 (Summer 1972).

78. His dithyrambic and wandering ruminations on Freud reveal considerable ambivalence about the Jewish intellectual father. See "The Father of the Psychoanalystic Movement" (1945), *Nature*, pp. 2–17. His review of Ernest Jones' biography holds that Freud withdrew from carrying out his ideas because of fear of conflict. *Nature*, p. 41. In "The Golden Age" he jumbled some Freudian metaphors in puzzlement over "the misery of resignation" instead of the Golden Age of our desires. *Nature*, pp. 18–29.

79. See the similar views decades later in *Speaking*.

80. In a good discussion of Goodman's psychology, Richard King rightly notes the rejection of much of Freud, the emphasis on im-

mediate situation, "unblocking," self-regulation, and the "peculiarly American flavor" of pragmatic problem-solving, the positive view of "creativity" and action (and, I would add, the belief in merging education and psychotherapy, as on p. 310), and the lack of the subtle, interior, and complex. *Party of Eros*, pp. 78–115. A rather different view is given by Theodore Roszak, who ignores the difficulties and exaggerates the role of the mystical. *The Making of a Counter Culture* (New York, 1969), pp. 186–98.

81. "Some Remarks on War Spirit," *Drawing the Line* (New York, 1962), pp. 78–85—long quote on p. 84.

82. *CP*, p. 135. When not engaging the social, Goodman often seems obtuse, as in the arbitrary and abstract analysis of an academic type in "On the Intellectual Inhibition of Physical Grief and Anger," *Nature*, pp. 179–92. As a therapist on "writing problems," he seems to have been reductive and rather ignorant about literary work, as in "On a Writer's Block," *Nature*, pp. 193–201. For an almost comical example of psyching literature, see "The Psychological Revolution and the Writer's Life-View," *Nature*, pp. 170–78.

83. See "Vocation and 'Public Conscience,' " *Line*, pp. 106–10. Related pieces on similar resistance seem quite hostile when not ambivalent: "Dear Graduate . . . ," and "To Young Resisters," *Line*, pp. 111–19. For the type of character Goodman was nervously responding to, see Austin Regier and Kingsley Widmer, *Why They Go to Prison* (Minneapolis, 1949).

84. See "On the Worldwide General Strike For Peace," *Line* (1962), pp. 90–96; "Declaring Peace Against the Governments," *Line*, pp. 120–26. There are other statements in *Liberation* in the 1960s. See also the novel *Making Do* (New York: Macmillan, 1963), passim.

85. Roszak, p. 184. In a typically uninsightful piece, Susan Sontag claims that Goodman had great influence on her. "On Paul Goodman," *New York Review of Books*, 19(Sept. 21, 1972), pp. 11–12. Henry Pachter, though inaccurately summarizing Goodman's ideas, more rightly emphasizes that he was not a good writer or original thinker but the practitioner of a "posture of dissent." "Paul Goodman—'Topian' Educator," *Salmagundi* 24(Fall 1973), 54–67. Goodman has been frequently cited by writers on marginal living, such as Ernest Callenbach, *Living Poor With Style* (New York, 1972).

86. These radical pacifists obviously had considerable influence on Goodman but he expresses ambivalence towards some of them, as evident in his preface to David McReynolds, *We Have Been Invaded by the 21st Century* (New York, 1970). For other activist

contrasts, see Jim Peck, *We Who Would Not Kill* (New York, 1964) and Dave Dellinger, *More Power Than We Know* (New York, 1975).

87. See *New Reformation*, passim. "I am squeamish about masses of people building a great society," *Little Prayers*, p. 77.

88. Quoted here from *Dissent* 9(Winter 1962), 6–22—reprinted in *Drawing the Line* (New York, 1962), pp. 55–77.

89. Goodman's public role seems to have changed his earlier positive views of subversion and bohemian withdrawal. He never had much sympathy for "moral witness" of Ghandians and others.

90. I am probably indebted here to the various writings of Ivan Illich, most recently *Toward a History of Needs* (New York, 1978).

91. *New Reformation*, p. 280. Jewish notions of the "saving remnant," neomedievalism, etc., could be sources, but some may be cruder.

92. *Province*, p. 19.

Chapter Four

1. After years of success as a social critic, he wrote of his literary efforts that such "writing is my free act," i.e., avocational. *Little Prayers*, p. 123.

2. The last section is titled "Book V," but Goodman later said there were only four. *Creator*, p. 254. He had elsewhere proposed a fifth book. *Creator*, p. 235. Later he published a bad story which a note identifies as a "further chapter" for Book V. *Adam and His Works* (New York, 1968), p. 372. Probably Goodman dallied off and on with doing some more of this shapeless, and therefore never clearly ended, work. He dropped the Preface (cited below) and changed subtitles and bits here and there. In some notes, he makes much of having substituted "peace" for "freedom," end of Bk. II, *The State of Nature*. *Five Years*, p. 218. But he was usually incapable of doing significant revision. Devotee Leo Raditsa reported that he spent "two years or so" trying to get the novel published but editors would "simply answer that man obviously could not write." *Iowa Review* 5(Summer 1974), p. 6. Norman Podhoretz claims to have arranged publication. *Making It* (New York, 1967), p. 296. Weirdly, Theodore Roszak viewed it as the work of Goodman's "guaranteed to endure." *The Making of a Counter Culture* (New York, 1969), p. 180.

3. *Five Years*, p. 172; see also his acknowledging lack of character development, p. 215; see also, for "cartoons," *Creator*, pp. 258–9. He explained the novel's ideology: "I find that *The Grand Piano* lays

great emphasis on the committee meetings of rational folk; the next book on the merging irrational idea when a crowd is stunned; the third on the erotic ideas of fraternal community; and the fourth on the rituals of natural functioning. . . ." *Creator*, p. 235. The fit is very bad. Richard King reasonably says that the novel is "nearly impossible to read" because of lack of character, poor visual sense, tin-ear dialogue, thinness and monotony. *Party of Eros* (Chapel Hill, N. C., 1972), pp. 204, 82–3.

4. "These news items are taken at random mostly from the issue of January 18, 1953." (Footnote, p. 501.)

5. In the dropped Preface, Goodman struck one amusingly defiant note: "I trust that there is nothing fundamentally unobjectionable." *Creator*, pp. 237–40. He also calls it a "comedy of sociological humors" and emphasizes much more than appears in the novel a source in Marx on "exchange values" (*Capital*, v. I, Ch. 24). He also wrote a sketch around this, "The Commodity Embodied in Bread," satirizing the fetishism of the packaging, parodying scholasticism, and ruminating on garbage. It is much less effective than Henry Miller's "Staff of Life."

6. As the late B. N. Nelson pointed out to me.

7. Sherman Paul, "Paul Goodman's Mourning Labor: The Empire City," holds that the novel was "a history of his friends." *Southern Review* 44(Oct. 1968), 897. This earnestly uncritical and long explication is the most elaborate attempt to take the work seriously, as an allegory of the educative-therapeutic for "natural satisfactions."

8. Including obsessional descriptions of fires, borrowed ideas (i.e., De Rougement on love of death), pseudo-Aristotelian ruminations (see p. 60), and vanguardist tidbits. Many of the more earnest notions also appear lumpishly elsewhere, as with boycotting superfluities, here and in "The Mean, The Maximum, and the Minimum," *Adam and His Works*, pp. 337–45.

9. Geoffrey Gardner misses the point in proclaiming the supposed descriptive qualities of this "master work." "Citizen of the World, Animal of Nowhere," *New Letters* 42 (Winter-Spring 1976), 216–27.

10. Nature, the text insists, restricts man from blowing up everything, but a footnote has been added: "Ha! So I thought in December 1944 . . ." (p. 265), a typical undercutting of fictional autonomy.

11. See "Revolution, Sociolatry, and War," *Art and Social Nature*.

12. See N. V. Riasnovsky, *The Teaching of Charles Fourier* (Berkeley, 1969). But it is mostly an example of Goodman's confessed "too much talking about" instead of showing. *Creator*, p. 256.

13. For exposition, see Chapter 5 of my *The Art of Perversity: D. H. Lawrence* (Seattle, 1962).

14. As Goodman's longtime friend, the late marginal writer William Poster, explained the coterie to me: "We are the ones who change culture."

15. While there isn't much merit in keeping the jumbled literal and allegorical lines straight, Lefty (the success) and Droyt—right and left hands?—are the sons of Laura (Horatio's sister, the architect and suicide), who is thus redeemed—the laurel of victory over despair?—and the "Good News" (gospel tidings?) announces a new bohemian ethos. Sherman Paul suggests that Goodman had "foreseen a new culture" and "the life style of the new generation," which is rather touching considering his actual antagonism to much of the 1960s bohemianism. *Southern Review*, p. 921.

16. Years later Goodman still calls this "a miracle." *Creator*, p. 266.

17. In a crudely told addition, "Laughing Laddy's Symbolic Act," *Adam and His Works*, pp. 372–83, the Irish figure copulates at Venice with a seventy-five-year-old beggar woman who then robs him, yet this provides the happy moral of "multiplying one's efforts, by latitudinarian standards, by being satisfied with modest successes." The author magnanimously recreated the experience, reported in *Five Years*, of sodomizing an old man.

18. Richard Kostelanetz, with usual critical incoherence, praises the novel while yet admitting it is "intolerably sloppy, lumpy . . . self-indulgent." *Master Minds* (New York, 1969), p. 285. That Goodman had no sense of the problems in his novels is further evident in his discussing minor grammatical matters, apparently as an escape from the real issues. *Five Years*, pp. 80–81.

19. There seems to be hardly any comment on *Parents' Day*.

20. And some pages, such as 109 ff., seem literally misordered in the two copies I have examined. The entitling episode, the school politics, the continuing lives, are thin and ill-focused. Repeated identifications of characters such as "Ross, the poet's son" (p. 120) when neither are otherwise present seems novelistically irresponsible.

21. And the usual conceit: "I, one of the good wits in America and a teacher by my artist-instinct . . ." (p. 87).

22. Possible autobiographical details will not be considered here.

23. In one of a series of unsuccessful Guggenheim applications, Goodman's project was this novel (1946); he emphasized that the "progressive educational community" is "not far from an ideal family." But perhaps to cover his negative treatment of the school,

he insists that some of it results from "the mad mores of the war-torn big world," though hardly any of this gets into the novel. *Creator,* p. 234.

24. The main building has burned down (the obsession with fires—sexual guilt?—has here a practical nexus). Building would express the community, but where the narrator wants functional huts, the powers want something more grandiloquent.

25. Stoehr has published the previously unpublished "Preface to the Fire (i.e., Parents' Day)." *Creator,* pp. 249–50. It claims that the work is about "the freedom of children," though "this ambivalent account" is necessary to understand the problems. In his last work, *Little Prayers,* he refers to parental love as *agape*—I suppose in the Anders Nygren sense (p. 99).

26. Art and utopianism merge for Goodman: "We artists always at once find ourselves a community, wherever the spontaneity of young people affords us a bridge" (p. 45)—but note the following parenthesis: "(but this community is, like our art, an imitation of happiness)." Intermittently, Goodman argued for communal art; at about the time of this novel he called for "Occasional Poetry" to celebrate communal events. *Creator,* pp. 75–78. "A Senior Orchestra" uses the high-school performance for ruminations on the process of community. *Adam and His Works,* pp. 346–50. Some of his verse aims to be "occasional" for his friends.

27. There are some suggestive pedagogical notions. The narrator learns "that one gains interest" from a student "not by showing heartfelt concern, but by doing something objective and to the point" (p. 36). This will later lead Goodman, contrary to vulgarized progressive education, to arguments for apprenticeships and traditional humanities. On communal psychodrama: children who saw a cow butchered and flayed, turn it into a ritual game. *Parents' Day,* 205–209. But elsewhere Goodman used the same incident for the opposite point—a "wise society ought to have a better expression" for accepting reality than such games. "Natural Violence" (1945), *Line,* p. 22. He moved towards communitarianism.

28. As indicated earlier in discussing *Communitas,* he reacts with a New Yorkerish rage rather than thought on flight from the cities, or the interesting possibility of abolishing such places as New York.

29. I am, of course, not questioning Goodman's sincerity, only his perceptivity. As he would undoubtedly agree, what is wrong with sociological theories of "role-playing" is that most people have to believe in what they do, the roles they assume—as does Goodman as pop-sociologist. For role-playing as "neurotic conformity," see

People, p. 134. As for sexual exploitation, see also the admission: "I do not care about/the young that I make love to." *CP,* p. 15.

30. He won't let the reader examine his claims. Even on one of the few negative examples—a speech by an establishment figure— he falls back on "I don't remember" what he said (p. 207) which may be appropriate to the substance, but is not a storyteller's response, and so we can't know. He is a bit better on a rough satire of conventional small city politics, curiously (pp. 131–39).

31. *Creator,* p. 255.

32. As he even later half-admitted: "I cannot really write fiction" (meaning the "imaginary"). *Little Prayers,* p. 31.

33. This self-selection "contains most of the contents of" *The Facts of Life* (1945), *The Break-Up of Our Camp* (1949), *Our Visit to Niagara* (1960), and "five new stories." In process are the *Collected Stories* in four volumes edited by Taylor Stoehr, of which I have seen only the first two: *The Break-Up of Our Camp, Stories 1932–1935* and *A Ceremonial, Stories 1936–1940* (Santa Barbara, Ca., 1978). All the additions, previously unpublished, seem poor or bad.

34. See "The Meaning of Abstraction in Literature" and "Preface to a Collection of Stories Never Published." *Creator,* pp. 10–20. 241–45.

35. Michael True, "Paul Goodman and the Triumph of American Prose Style," *New Letters,* 42(Winter-Spring 1976), 228–36, makes similar points. The irony in the title, incidentally, doesn't seem intentional but refers to the best of the plain-spoken social criticism. For other views of the stories, see David Ray's "Preface" to the above issue: Goodman was "not a *good* writer . . . but a great one" (p. 6). Stoehr's "Introduction" says of Goodman's stories that "they are among the finest in our literature" (p. 9). John J. Enck examined one of Goodman's better efforts, "The Architect from New York," and pointed out its smug "parochial vantage point," its inconsistency, its lack of dramatization, its confusion of tone, and the bad writing *Wisconsin Studies in Contemporary Literature* 1(Fall 1960), 96 ff.

36. I think the earlier version is clearer for my purposes, and so I am quoting *Collected Stories,* I, p. 194, instead of Goodman's shortened version in *Adam and His Works,* p. 154.

37. This is one of the few to have been anthologized several times. The style is so at variance with what Goodman usually does that one suspects collaboration or a strong editorial hand.

38. See also "Terry Fleming," a wandering, stilted, and cute sketch concluding with "Hints on Planning a Universe," which anti-

Jewishly repeats three times *"Don't* have any 'chosen people,' "
Adam and His Works, pp. 30–31.

39. *Adam and His Works,* pp. 360–71. But other travel pieces are
bad. See "A Visit to Chartres," (pp. 172–81). This pontificating piece
loosely describes an ecstatic response, though he is upset at the
too small square; "these feelings plus my usual effortful and earnest
aesthetic and sociological reflections"—such as "How big and
manly!"

40. *Adam and His Works,* pp. 412–19. For the Irish trip, see
Five Years.

41. Kostelanetz reports that the 1959 production of *Cave at
Machpelah* was "cruelly reviewed." *Master Minds,* p. 284.

42. A production of Trojan Women is described in *Parents' Day.*

43. *Parents' Day,* p. 135. See also "Art of the Theatre," *Three
Plays* (New York, 1964), p. xviii; and "The Drama of Awareness,"
Stop-Light (Harrington Park, N. J., 1941).

44. The same material was used in a bad ruminative sketch,
"The Minutes Are Flying By Like A Snowstorm," published posthumously in *New Letters,* 113–21. He was scared in an old car.

45. *Three Plays,* pp. 131–200 (first printed in *Facts of Life,*
1945). He comments elsewhere, "Jonah is the prophet of the philosophy that Jews call *Nebichism* . . . the conviction that 'everything
goes from bad to worse.' " *Creator,* p. 228. He also published a cute
piece of juvenilia, *Childish Jokes: Crying Backstage* (New York,
1938); ". . . hear a dirty joke? The boy fell in the mud." *Jonah,*
performed by New York's American Place Theatre (February 1966),
has much the same quality.

46. *Three Plays,* pp. 63–130 (dated 1948). As Goodman admitted
in a tonally garbled story, "Trying to be archaic, I get pedantic."
"A Ceremonial," *Adam and His Works,* p. 45.

47. He cites Artaud, anyway, in 1955 (*Five Years,* p. 43.) For
his mixed responses to Artaud, see "Obsessed by Theatre," *Creator,*
pp. 111–5.

48. *Three Plays,* p. vii.

49. "Notes on Abraham," *Response* (Spring-Summer 1970), 59–
61. *Abraham and Isaac* appeared in *i. e., The Cambridge Review*
1(Nov. 1955), 216–230; *Hagar and Ishmael* in *Response* (Spring-
Summer 1970), 49–59; *The Cave at Machpelah* in *Commentary* 25
(June 1958), 512–517. A fourth appears not to have been pub-
lished. When he talks of other biblical dramas going back to 1935
(*Creator,* p. 229), he may be pointing to two slight earlier playlets,
"The Tower of Babel," *New Directions in Prose and Poetry,* v. 5

(New York, 1940), pp. 19–38, and "Cain and Abel," *Five Young American Poets* (New York, 1941), pp. 9–25.

50. Conversation with Nelson; see also *New Reformation*, p. 207.

51. With two exceptions, noted below, I am using *CP*. It does not include much of the earlier work found in *Ten Lyric Poems* (New York, 1934), *12 Ethical Sonnets* (New York, 1935), *15 Poems With Time Expressions* (New York, 1936), *A Warning at My Leisure* (Harrington Park, N. J: 1939), a number of privately printed booklets and some periodical publications. Larger collections, repetitive, include *The Lordly Hudson* (New York, 1962), *Hawkweed* (New York, 1967), and *Homespun of Oatmeal Gray* (New York, 1970).

52. Few of these exercises seem interesting to me; best perhaps are "Ballade of Difficult Arrangements" (*CP*, p. 252) the Anacreaon imitation "Solstice" (*CP*, p. 256), and the neatly sour little epigram "A Meal" (*CP*, p. 383). For an opposite view of Goodman's poetry, and general praise, see Richard Howard, *Alone with America* (New York, 1969), pp. 153–63.

53. A very few times he recognizes, and goes for, the burlesque effect of his oddity and forcing, as in his couplet on traditional Navy seaman's dress: "a lad couldn't have a hard-on but it showed/and his behind rippled as he goed" (*CP*, p. 259).

54. This includes some of the points Goodman emphasizes in "Defence of Poetry" (*Speaking*). He recognized and praised (except what contradicted his nasty male chauvinism) some of what Williams was doing in "The Flash and the Thunderstroke." *Creator*, pp. 213–17.

55. There is confusion in Goodman's sense of poetical inversion. He claims that "poets contrive to make interjections an organic part of their language by inverting the word order . . ." *Speaking*, p. 39. But interjection is often not inversion, and Goodman's inversions are often not interjections, just "poetical" triteness.

56. The sequence varies with publication—110 instead of 92 in the volume entitled *Little Prayers*. In its preface, he admits that "I otherwise never use" this religious jargon and it is just "poetic license." Role-playing or obtuseness? See also pp. 121–22.

57. About the same time he also wrote: I "cannot pray in any usual sense, though I sometimes use the awareness exercises of psychotherapy which, I guess, is my religion," *Speaking*, p. 238. He does pray to "Nature" in an awkward little piece about his sick daughter (*CP*, p. 385). I am not denying religious muddle, as evident in the mixed agnostic, Calvinistic, Taoistic, and perhaps covert Judaistic, ruminations in *Little Prayers*, pp. 79 ff., but the emphasis

is on "finite" and points most essential to an agnostically utilitarian view of religion.

58. No doubt various "expressive fallacies" could also be suggested, as with mechanical moan-indicators ("ai, ai") to weakly conclude "Philoctetes" (*CP*, p. 381). He repeatedly did this mechanical stuff in his stage business, also. Perhaps a more appropriate religious expression would be the creation when "Brahma/splattered jerking off/with for his bride/the Void." *CP*, p. 397.

59. A different way of putting this is that the imposed poetical patterns "never quite fit." Michael True, *New Letters*, p. 233. Richard King agrees that the poetry is "distinctly inferior to his social criticism," and is "wooden and windy." *Party of Eros*, p. 82. The changes in "The Lordly Hudson"—"Be quiet heart!" to "Be patient, Paul!"—are, as with most of his revisions, unimportant personal variations.

60. Some of this, of course, appears in the prose—the call for a statue to himself in the introduction to *Three Plays*, p. xvii.

61. There are many examples of this insistent male nastiness. See the attempt at a sonnet using Milton's notorious line "He for God Only, She For God In Him." *CP*, p. 278. Or, in commenting on women college students, he dismisses them as "girls who needed babies." *CP*, p. 340.

62. For the verbal becoming compensatory sexual defense, see *CP*, pp. 247, 412.

63. Sometimes he touchingly recognized why he demanded the adulation of the young in the 1960s: "Thwarted as a man/I grew deluded about my importance/because teen-agers look to me for words" (*CP*, p. 347).

64. So with Emile Capouya. For praise of the verse for no very good reason, see his "The Poet as Prophet," *Parnassus* (Fall-Winter 1974), pp. 23–30; or Neil Heims, "Who Sang the Lordly Hudson" *Nation* (June 29, 1974), pp. 824–26. More appropriately, in a survey Kenneth Rexroth praises Goodman for his enduring libertarianism (in contrast to other intellectuals of his New York ambience), but says nothing of the verse. *American Poetry in the Twentieth Century* (New York, 1971), pp. 134–35.

65. I have restored the classically adapted title, inexplicably dropped in *CP*, that was used in *North Percy* (Los Angeles, 1968), p. 1.

66. I have changed back one word—"marrow" for "chicken" (bone)—following the version in *Little Prayers* (p. 76), since the connotations of marrow seem better (and less mean to the dog).

Selected Bibliography

PRIMARY SOURCES

(Only Paul Goodman's more substantial books are listed. An asterisk preceding the title indicates that the edition was in print when this book went to press. Many of his numerous periodical contributions have been collected or revised for publication in the books. For a tentative list of all his publications up to the time of his death, see Eliot Glassheim, "Paul Goodman: A Checklist, 1931–1971," *Bulletin of Bibliography* 29 [April-June 1972], 61–72. Most of his important periodical pieces are also mentioned in the notes to this book.)

1. Collected Works

*Collected Poems. New York: Random House, 1973; Vintage (paper), 1974 (abbreviated *CP* in text and notes).
*Collected Stories, ed. Taylor Stoehr. Volume 1: *The Break-Up of Our Camp: Stories 1932–1935*; Volume 2: *A Ceremonial: Stories 1936–1940*. Santa Barbara: Black Sparrow Press, 1978. (Two more volumes announced.)
*Creator Spirit Come!: The Literary Essays of Paul Goodman, ed. Taylor Stoehr. New York: Free Life Editions, 1977 (abbreviated *Creator* in text and notes).
*Drawing the Line: The Political Essays of Paul Goodman. Ed. Taylor Stoehr. New York: Free Life Editions, 1977 (abbreviated *Line* in text and notes).
*Nature Heals: The Psychological Essays of Paul Goodman. Ed. Taylor Stoehr. New York: Free Life Editions, 1977 (abbreviated *Nature* in text and notes).

2. Novels

The Empire City. Indianapolis: Bobbs-Merrill, 1959. Contains as Parts I, II, and III revised versions of *The Grand Piano: or, The Almanac of Alienation*. San Francisco: Colt Press, 1942; *The State of Nature*. New York: Vanguard, 1946; and *The Dead of Spring*. Glen Gardner, N.J.: Liberation Press, 1950. *Reprinted (paper): New York: Macmillan, 1964.

Making Do. New York: Macmillan, 1963. Reprinted (paper): New York: New American Library, 1964.
Parents' Day (with illustrations by Percival Goodman). Saugatuck, Conn.: 5x8 Press, 1951.

3. Stories and Sketches

Adam and His Works. New York: Vintage, 1969.
The Break-Up of Our Camp and Other Stories. Norfolk, Conn.: New Directions, 1949.
The Facts of Life. New York: Vanguard, 1945.
Our Visit to Niagara. New York: Horizon, 1960.

4. Plays

Stop-Light (with drawings by Percival Goodman). Harrington Park, N.J.: 5x8 Press, 1941.
Three Plays: The Young Disciple, Faustina, Jonah. New York: Random House, 1965.
Tragedy & Comedy: Four Cubist Plays. Los Angeles: Black Sparrow, 1970.

5. Poems (larger collections other than *CP*).

Hawkweed. New York: Random House/Vintage, 1967.
Homespun of Oatmeal Gray. New York: Random House/Vintage, 1970.
The Lordly Hudson. New York: Macmillan, 1962.

6. Essays

Art and Social Nature. New York: Vinco, 1946.
Communitas—Means of Livelihood and Ways of Life, with Percival Goodman. Chicago: Univ. of Chicago Press, 1947. *Revised edition (paper): New York: Random House/Vintage, 1960.
The Community of Scholars. New York: Random House, 1962 (see also next entry).
Compulsory Mis-education. New York: Horizon, 1964. Reprinted with *The Community of Scholars* (paper): New York: Random House/Vintage, 1966 (abbreviated as *Scholars* and *Compulsory* in text and notes).
Drawing the Line. New York: Random House, 1962.
Five Years: Thoughts During a Useless Time. New York: Brussel and Brussel, 1966. Reprinted (paper): New York: Vintage, 1969.

Gestalt Therapy: Excitement and Growth in the Human Personality,
with Frederick Perls and Ralph Hefferline. New York: Julian
Press, 1951. Reprinted (paper): New York: Dell, n.d.

Growing Up Absurd—Problems of Youth in the Organized Society.
New York: Random House, 1960; Vintage (paper), 1962
(abbreviated as *Absurd* in text and notes).

Kafka's Prayer. New York: Vanguard, 1947. *Reprinted: New York:
Stonehill, 1976.

Like a Conquered Province—The Moral Ambiquity of America. New
York: Random House, 1967. Reprinted with *People or Personnel*
(paper): New York: Vintage, 1968 (abbreviated as *Province*
in text and notes).

Little Prayers and Finite Experience. New York: Harper and Row,
1972.

New Reformation—Notes of a Neolithic Conservative. New York:
Random House, 1970.

People or Personnel—Decentralizing and the Mixed System. New
York: Random House, 1965. See also *Like a Conquered Province,* above (abbreviated as *People* in text and notes).

The Society I Live In Is Mine. New York: Horizon, 1963 (abbreviated as *Society* in text and notes).

Speaking and Language. New York: Random House, 1971 (abbreviated as *Speaking* in text and notes).

The Structure of Literature. Chicago: Univ. of Chicago Press, 1954.
*Reprinted (paper): Chicago: Phoenix Books, 1962).

Utopian Essays and Practical Proposals. New York: Random House,
1962. Reprinted (paper): New York: Vintage, 1962 (abbreviated as *Utopian* in text and notes).

SECONDARY SOURCES

(Only the more important articles are listed; for many other materials see the Notes and References.)

KING, RICHARD. "Paul Goodman" in *The Party of Eros.* Chapel Hill,
N.C.: Univ. of North Carolina Press, 1972, pp. 78–115. A
sensibly balanced discussion of some of Goodman's social
thought, with an emphasis on his use of psychology in the context of American Left-Freudianism.

ROSZAK, THEODORE. "Exploring Utopia: The Visionary Sociology of
Paul Goodman" in *The Making of a Counter Culture.* New
York: Doubleday, 1969, pp. 178–204. An evangelizing account

of some of Goodman's social ideology which has had considerable popular influence.

STOEHR, TAYLOR. Introductions to *Creator Spirit Come!*, *Drawing the Line*, and *Nature Heals*. All New York: Free Life Editions, 1977. These introductions to a three-volume selection of Goodman's literary, political, and psychological essays constitute (with the headnotes in the text) an informative though uncritical monograph.

TRUE, MICHAEL. "Paul Goodman and the Triumph of American Prose Style." *New Letters* (Special Goodman double issue) 42 (Winter/Spring 1976), 228–36. Though mistitled, this is a sensible criticism of Goodman's bad literary work and good social thought.

WIDMER, KINGSLEY. *The Literary Rebel*. Carbondale: Southern Illinois Univ. Press, 1965, pp. 186–98. One of the earliest broad accounts of Goodman, continued in *The End of Culture*. San Diego: San Diego State Univ. Press, 1975, pp. 116–22.

Index

Alexander, Franz, 91
Anders, Gunther, 29
Arendt, Hannah, 86
Aristotle, 25, 26, 27, 28, 29, 72, 73, 76
Arnold, Matthew, 25, 58
Artaud, Antoine, 134, 173
Atlas, James, 151

Baudelaire, Charles, 27
Baukunin, Michael, 60, 154
Bell, Daniel, 158
Bellamy, Edward, 156
Berkman, Alexander, 155
Blake, William, 28, 42, 95
Blanc, Louis, 47
Borsodi, Ralph, 43, 45, 85
Brown, Norman O., 91, 156
Bruner, Jerome, 163
Buber, Martin, 18, 32, 33, 110, 165

Calhoun, Donald, 93, 165
Callenback, Ernest, 167
Capouya, Emile, x., 175
Catullus, 27
Céline, L.-F., 82
Chuang-tzu, 110, 114
Chomsky, Noam, 32, 33, 34
Clair, René, 27
Cocteau, Jean, 31, 31, 110
Cohen, Morris R., xv
Coleridge, S. T., 58
Corneille, Pierre, 27

Dellinger, David, 100, 168
Dennison, George, 110, 151, 161
De Rougement, Denis, 169
Dewey, John, 72, 73, 83, 161, 165
Dickstein, Morris, 153

Diogenes (Cynics), 38, 64
Dryden, John, 27
Duberman, Martin, 161
Durkheim, Emile, 98

Ehrlich, H. and C., 154
Eisenhower, Dwight D., 108
Ellul, Jacques, 86
Enck, John J., 160
Epstein, Joseph, 153

Faraday, Michael, 84
Faulkner, William, 98
Feurer, Lewis S., 160
Flaubert, Gustave, 27
Fourier, Charles, 114, 169
French, Warren, xii-xiii, 153
Freud, Sigmund (and Freudianism), 29, 30, 41, 42, 91-99, 111, 165, 166
Friedenberg, Edgar A., 161
Fromm, Erich, 91
Fuller, Buckminster, 43, 156

Gardner, Geoffrey, 169
Genet, Jean, 23, 31, 72, 140
Gide, Andre, 110, 121
Ginsberg, Alan, 30, 31, 69, 73
Godwin, William, 73
Goethe, W., 110, 117
Goldsmith, Oliver, 129
Goodman, Alice, xv, 18, 20
Goodman, Augusta, xv, 18, 19
Goodman, Lawrence, 158
Goodman, Mathew, xvi, xvii, 61, 142
Goodman, Paul,
    WRITINGS:
    Adam and His Works, 126-32, 170, 171-73

180

"Advance-Guard Writing in America: 1900-1950," 31

"A. J. Muste and People in Power," 100

"Anarchism and Revolution," 60-61, 158, 159

"The Anarchists," 155

"'Applied Science' and Superstition," 84-85

"April 1966," 139

"An April Walk," 139

"The Architect from New York," 172

Art and Social Nature ("The May Pamphlet"), 38-42

"Art of the Theatre," 132

"The Attempt to Invent an American Style," 152

"Ballads of Difficult Arrangements," 174

"Banning Cars from Manhattan," 87

"On Being a Writer," 20

"Berkeley in February," 71

"Between the Flash and the Thunderstroke," 137, 174

"The Birthday," 133

"Black Flag," 63-64

"The Black Flag of Anarchism," 58-60, 158

The Break-Up of Our Camp, 130, 172

"Cain and Abel," 174

"A Causerie at the Military-Industrial," 102

"The Chance for Popular Culture," 88, 165

"A Chess Game," 139

Childish Jokes, 173

"The Children and Psychology," 160

"A Christmas Tree," 139

"A Classical Quatrain," 139

Collected Poems, 136-43, 174-75

"Commencement, 1962," 175

Communitas, 42-49, 58, 145, 146, 156, 157

The Community of Scholars, 73-84, 161, 162, 163, 164

Compulsory Mis-education, 74, 75, 76, 77, 78-84, 162, 163, 164

"Confusion and Disorder," 62-63

"A Conjecture in American History," 158

"Crisis and New Spirit," 71

The Dead of Spring, 107, 114-16

"Dear Graduate . . . .," 99

"The Death of Aesculapius," 130

"Declaring Peace Against the Governments," 99, 167

"The Detective Story," 127

"The Devolution of Democracy," 100-101

"A Diary of Makapuu," 139

"Diggers in 1984," 158

Drawing the Line (see *Art and Social Nature*), 38-42, 100-101, 102, 145, 146

"The Dream of Awareness," 143

"Dusk," 133

"The Duty of Professionals," 102-104

"The Education Industries," 80

The Empire City, 37, 106-18, 122, 129, 152, 168-70

"The Facts of Life," 128

The Family of Abraham (*Abraham and Isaac, Hagar and Ishmael, The Cave at Machpelah*), 134, 173

"The Father of the Psychoanalytic Movement," 96, 166

Faustina, 134

Five Years, 18, 151, 152, 153, 155, 160, 161, 168, 170

"Format and Anxiety," 34, 164

"The Formulation of Freedom," 159

"Foster excellence . . . ," 139

"Four Little Prayers," 140

Freedom and Order in the University, 74, 159, 161, 162

"The Freedom to be Academic," 161

"From John Dewey to A. S. Neill,"
73, 161
"The Galley to Mytilence," 130
Gestalt Therapy, 21, 79, 92-97,
114, 145, 146, 163, 165, 166
"The Golden Age," 18, 96, 166
The Grand Piano, 72, 107, 109-11,
168
"The Great Bear in the tingling
sky," 139
"Great Pioneer, but No Libertar-
ian," 165
Growing Up Absurd, 58, 65-70,
71, 146, 153, 160, 161
The Holy Terror, 107-109, 116-18
"A Hustler," 141, 142
"Iddings Clark," 130-31
"The Ineffectuality of Some Intel-
ligent People," 101-102
"An Interview on The Empire
City," 169-70
"Introduction to Prison Memoirs of
an Anarchist," 155
"Jeremy Owen," 131
Jonah, 133-34
"June and July," 136-37, 140, 141
"In the Jury Room, In Pain," 142
Kafka's Prayer, 28-9, 146, 156
"La Gaya Scienza," 141, 142
"[Last Public Speech]," 78
Like a Conquered Province, 57-58,
85, 98, 105, 145, 146, 156, 157,
168
"Lilacs," 140
"Lines . . . ," 139
"Literary Method and Author-At-
titude," 106
Little Prayers and Finite Experi-
ence, 72, 84, 137-38, 154, 155,
157, 159, 161, 164, 165, 166,
168, 172, 174
"Long Lines on the Left Bank,"
142
"The Lordly Hudson," 138, 175
"Low Tide," 142
Making Do, 38, 122-26, 154, 167,

171, 172
Mass Education in Science, 162
"The May Pamphlet" (Art and So-
cial Nature, Drawing the Line),
38-42
"A Meal," 174
"The Meaning of Abstraction in
Literature," 126, 172
"The Minutes Are Flying By Like
A Snowstorm," 173
"The Moral Idea of Money," 153
"The Morality of Scientific Tech-
nology," 85
"Morning," 141
"My Daughter Very Ill," 174
"Natural Violence" (Art and So-
cial Nature), 40, 171
"Neo-Classicism, Platonism, and
Romanticism," 25-26
"A New Deal for the Arts," 89, 165
"A New Directive from the Penta-
gon," 174
New Reformation, 35-36, 56-57,
58, 61-62, 73, 74, 75, 77, 78,
79, 85-87, 99-100, 104, 145, 146,
156, 158, 160, 161, 162, 163,
168
"New Theatre and the Unions," 88
"New York," 139
"No image or idea," 175
North Percy, 175
"Notes on Decentralization," 52
"Notes on Neo-Functionalism," 157
"Occasional Poetry," 171
"The Old Knight," 131
"On Being a Writer . . . ," 151
"On the Sonnet," 140
"On the Intellectual Inhibition of
Explosive Grief and Anger," 91,
167
The Open Look, 164
"Our Standard of Living," 159
"Our Visit to Niagara," 128-29,
146
"Pagan Rites," 142
Parents' Day, 19, 72, 118, 122,
170-71, 173

People or Personnel, 51-56, 146

"Perseus," 172

"Philocletes," 175

"Poems of a Heart Attack," 137

"The Political Meaning of Some Recent Revisions of Freud," 91-92

"The Politics of Being Queer," 151-52

"Pornography and the Sexual Revolution," 89-90

"Post-Christian Man," 160

"Power Struggles," 100

"A Pragmatic Love Song," 139

"Preface to *The Grand Piano*," 169

"[Preface to *Parents' Day*]," 171

"Preface to *We Have Been Invaded by the 21st Century*," 167

"The Present Moment in Education," 72-83

"My Psychology as a 'Utopian Sociologist'," 166

"The Psychological Revolution and the Writer's Life-View," 153, 167

"The Psychology of Being Powerless," 98

"A Public Dream of Universal Disaster," 75, 166

"To a Question of Helen Duberstein," 140

"Reading *Weepers Tower*," 142

"Dr. Reich's Banned Books," 92, 165

"Review of *On the Road*," 30, 67

"Reflections On the Anarchist Principle," 49-50

"Reflections on Drawing the Line" (*Art and Social Nature*), 39

"Reflections on Racism, Spite, Guilt and Non-Violence," 98-99

"The Relation of Culture and Learning," 161-62

"Revolution, Sociolatry, and War," ("The May Pamphlet"), 40-41, 170

"Rural Life: 1984," 51

"Schultz, the neighbor's big black dog," 142-43, 175

"Sciences and Professions," 85-87

"Seating Arrangements," 164

"A Senior Orchestra," 171

"Sentences," 139

"Sentences for Mathew Ready" (Series I and II), 139, 140, 141, 142

"September 9, 1964," 143

"Sex and Ethics," 166

"Sex and Revolution," 165

"The Shape of the Screen," 165

The Society I Live in Is Mine, 159, 160, 163, 164, 165

"Solstice," 174

"Some Problems of Interpretation, Silence, and Speech as Action," 30

"Some Remarks On War Spirit," 97-98, 167

Speaking and Language, 31-36, 137, 146, 153, 154, 166, 174

The State of Nature, 107, 111-14

"A Statue of Goldsmith," 129-30, 146

"A Statue of Nestor," 130

Stop-Light, 132-33

"The Stop-Light," 133

The Structure of Literature, 25-28

"Sycamores," 139

"Television: The Continuing Disaster," 87-88

"Terry Fleming," 172-73

"There is spring in my new shoes," 141

"The 3 Disciplines," 133

"Though I have gone to Glendalough," 139

"Thoughts on Fever," 151

Three Plays, 133-34

"A Touchstone for the Libertarian Program" ("The May Pamphlet"), 40

"Tower of Babel," 173

Tragedy and Comedy ("Structure of Tragedy, *after Aeschylus*"; "Structure of Tragedy, *after Sophocles*"; "Structure of Pathos, *after Euripides*"; "Little Hero, *after Moliere*"), 135-36

"On Treason Against Natural Societies" ("The May Pamphlet"), 39

[TV Columns], 164-65

"Two Points of Philosophy and an Example," 50-51

"Unanimity" ("The May Pamphlet"), 41-42

"Underground Writing: 1960," 31

"Urbanization and Rural Reconstruction," 157

Utopian Essays and Practical Proposals, 30, 70, 71, 90, 145, 153, 154, 160, 164

"Utopian Thinking," 90-91

"A Visit to Chartres," 173

"Vocational Guidance," 70

"Vocation and 'Public Conscience'," 99, 167

"Waters and Skies," 139

"Western Traditions and World Concern," 30

"Wild Glad Hours," 139

"Wordsworth's Poems," 30, 153

"Writer's Block," 167

The Young Disciple, 134

"To Young Resisters," 99, 167

"For a Young Widow," 142, 175

"Youth Work Camps," 70

Goodman, Percival, xv, xvi, 42ff., 87

Grogan, Emmett ("Diggers"), 58, 59, 158

Gross, Ronald and Beatrice, 161

Hardin, Sam, xii, 165

Harrington, Michael, 158

Hawthorne, Nathaniel, 27, 130

Heims, Neil, 175

Hefferline, Ralph, 92

Heller, Erich, 29

Hemingway, Ernest, 31, 154, 166

Hesse, Herman, 117

Hofstader, Richard, 158

Holt, John, 161, 164

Horney, Karen, 91

Howard, Ebenezer, 43, 156

Howard, Richard, 174

Howe, Irving, 152

Humphrey, Hubert, 108

Huxley, Aldous, 35

Illich, Ivan, 50, 85, 161, 164, 168

James, William, 112

Jefferson, Thomas, 23, 57, 60, 61, 73, 100, 155

Jencks, Christopher, 162

Job, Book of, 30

Jonson, Ben, 27

Joyce, James, 30

Kafka, Franz, 23, 27, 28-29, 72, 110, 153, 163

Kant, Immanuel, 18, 61, 155, 163

Kazin, Alfred, 151, 154

Kennedy, John F., 69, 100-101, 152

Kerouac, Jack, 30, 67, 69

Kierkegaard, Soren, 135

King, Richard, 152, 155, 157, 166, 167, 169, 175

Klee, Paul, 110, 142

Koehler, Wolfgang, 92

Kostelantz, Richard, 151, 170, 173

Kropotkin, Peter, 23, 45, 59, 60, 154, 165

Kuhn, Thomas, 86

Lao-tzu (Taoism), 62, 94, 114, 165

Lauter, Paul (and Howe, Florence), 162

Lawrence, D. H., x, 89, 110, 116, 169

Leavis, F. R., 25

Le Corbusier, 44

Lenin, V. I. (Leninism), 58, 104

Lipset, Seymour, 158

Living Theatre (Beck-Malina), xvi, 132, 134

Longinus, 25
Lowen, Alexander, 92, 94, 108
Lynd, Staughton, 100

McKeon, Richard, 25
MacDonald, Dwight (*Politics*), ix, 24, 38, 40, 41, 152
MacLeish, Archibald, 112
McReynolds, David, 100, 167
Mailer, Norman, 91, 123, 124, 149, 160, 165, 166
Malamud, Bernard, 131, 149
Mann, Thomas, 111
Marcuse, Herbert, 91, 94, 156, 165
Marx, Karl (Marxism), 37, 40, 41, 59, 67, 77, 91, 160, 169
Mazzocco, Robert, 151
Michels, Robert, 54
Miller, Henry, x, 154, 169
Miller, Virginia, xv
Milton, John, 23, 30, 58, 73, 175
Monet, Claude, 131
Moore, Barrington, Jr., 157
Mumford, Lewis, 85, 156
Muste, A. J., 100

Neill, A. S., 45, 73, 161
Nelson, Benjamin N., xii, 110, 136, 169, 174
Nietzsche, Frederick, 25

Orwell, George, 35

Pachter, Henry, 167
Parsons, Talcott, 66
Paul, Sherman, 169, 170
Peck, Jim, 168
Perls, F. S., xvi, 92, 165
Perls, Lore, 92
Plato, 25, 43, 124, 125, 157
Podhoretz, Norman, 24, 160, 168
Poggioli, Renato, 154
Pollack, Norman, 157
Poster, William, 170
Proudhon, Pierre, 63, 159

Raditsa, Leo, 151, 168

Rank, Otto, 91, 110
Ransom, John Crowe, 30, 31, 137
Ray, David, 172
Reich, Wilhelm, 45, 72, 90, 91-92, 94, 97, 113, 118, 121, 149, 165
Reimer, Everett, 161
Rexroth, Kenneth, 175
Riasnovsky, N. V., 169
Riesman, David, 156
Rilke, Rainer, M., 110
Rorem, Ned, 152
Rosenblatt, Daniel, 160
Roszak, Theodore, 167, 168
Rousseau, J.-J. (Rousseauism), 40, 61, 73, 95, 155

Salinger, J. D., xii
Santayana, George, 110
Sartre, Jean-Paul, 19, 25
Schlesinger, Arthur, Jr., 101
Schumacher, E. F., 56, 86
Schwartz, Delmore, 110, 151
Shakespeare, William, 26, 27, 68, 153
Shepard, Martin, 165
Silverman, H. J., 158
Skinner, B. F., 32
Smith, Adam, 49-50
Snow, C. P., 86
Solotaroff, Theodore, 152
Sophocles, 26
Spinoza, Baruch, 153
Spock, Benjamin, 62
Steiner, George, 153
Stoehr, Taylor, xi, 152, 153, 160, 165

Tennyson, Alfred, 27
Theobald, Robert, 157
Thoreau, Henry David, 62, 155
Tillyard, E. M., 26
Trotsky, Leon, 25
Tolstoy, Leo, 73, 154
Trilling, Lionel, 149
True, Michael, 172, 175

Veblen, Thorstein, 67, 73, 104

Wagner, Richard, 111

Ward, Colin, 155, 156
Washington, George, 68
West, Nathanael, 31, 111
Weber, Max, 67, 76, 96
Whyte, William H., 66
Widmer, Eleanor Rackow, x, xi, 18, 24
Wieck, David, 155

Williams, Penny, xii, 150
Williams, William Carlos, 137
Wolff, Robert Paul, 156
Woodcock, George, 154
Wordsworth, William, 30, 110, 141, 153
Wright, Frank Lloyd, 43, 45

Zamiatin, Eugene, 35